Praise for *Celtic Goddess Grimoire*

"*Celtic Goddess Grimoire* is a fascinating decoction steeped in folklore, history, mythology, and archaeology. Infused with sacred practices, meditations, and rituals, it is a must read for anyone seeking to cultivate a meaningful relationship with the divine feminine across the Celtic landscape."

—Danielle Blackwood, author of *The Twelve Faces of the Goddess* and *A Lantern in the Dark*

"Overflowing with a magical and inspiring spirit like the cauldrons of ancient lore, *Celtic Goddess Grimoire* is the kind of book I wish I had while growing into my own path as a young Pagan. From the hands-on, practical exercises, which enable you to build a real, embodied working relationship with these goddesses to the informative explorations of lore and myth, this book provides you with a deeply firm foundation. From this foundation, your practice can only flower and evolve with time. Accessible, thorough, and refreshing, this book is one I highly recommend for those who feel the call of the goddesses of the Celts. An absolute pleasure to read from start to finish."

—Mhara Starling, author of *Welsh Witchcraft*

"Annwyn Avalon has written an appealing and informative handbook which will prove immensely valuable to all those fascinated by goddesses of the Celtic lands. Both beginners and experienced practitioners alike will learn about each deity and discover how to forge a strong connection with them through unique and engaging meditations, rituals, and magical activities. An inspirational offering!"

—Mara Freeman, author of *Kindling the Celtic Spirit* and *Grail Alchemy*

"*Celtic Goddess Grimoire* is a rare delight that helps bring the goddesses of the ancient Celtic world into the lives of the next generation. With exercises and spells attached to each goddess, readers will find plenty of information to assist them in their magical practice whilst learning more about the importance of the Divine Feminine. This beautiful work by Annwyn Avalon blends the knowledge of the past with a life lived in modern magic. By merging history with the cyclic life of a priestess, she creates rare gems that balance history with spirituality; helping every reader to reconnect with these goddesses and, through them, to themselves. Life can be hectic and draining, but this beautiful book brings the mysteries from the past into a comprehensive modern book."

—Joey Morris, author of *Crow Speak Anthology: The Morrigan* and proprietor of Starry Eyed Supplies

"*Celtic Goddess Grimoire* by Annwyn Avalon is just what I would want in a book of this type—thorough, thoughtful, approachable, well-researched, practical, and divinely inspired. Its pages are packed with friendly guidance, historical insights, and authentic connection with the sacred women of Celtic lore. With this work, Annwyn offers readers a book that is part historical reference guide and part practical grimoire. It is a must have for any practitioner of Celtic spirituality!"

—Laurelei Black, author of *Aphrodite's Priestess* and the Red Thread Academy course guides

CELTIC GODDESS
GRIMOIRE

*Invoke the Enduring Power of the
Celtic Feminine Divine*

ANNWYN AVALON

WEISER BOOKS

This edition first published in 2024 by Weiser Books, an imprint of
Red Wheel/Weiser, LLC

With offices at:
65 Parker Street, Suite 7
Newburyport, MA 01950
www.redwheelweiser.com

Library of Congress Cataloging-in-Publication Data

Names: Avalon, Annwyn, 1983- author.
Title: Celtic goddess grimoire : invoke the enduring power of the Celtic feminine divine /
Annwyn Avalon.
Description: Newburyport, MA : Weiser Books, 2024. | Includes bibliographical references and
   index. | Summary: "The history, symbolism, and enduring power of the Celtic goddesses—
   with rituals and   exercises to celebrate, honor, invoke, and serve these sacred beings"
   Provided by publisher.
Identifiers: LCCN 2023044415 | ISBN 9781578638024 (trade paperback) |
   ISBN 9781633413023 (ebook)
Subjects: LCSH: Goddesses, Celtic. | Mythology, Celtic. | Magic. | Incantations. | BISAC:
   BODY, MIND & SPIRIT / Celtic Spirituality | BODY, MIND & SPIRIT / Witchcraft
   (see also RELIGION / Wicca)
Classification: LCC BL473.5 A97 2024 | DDC 299/.1612114—dc23/eng/20231204
LC record available at https://lccn.loc.gov/2023044415

Cover design and art by Sky Peck Design
Cover art adapted from the public domain work *Tristan and Isolde*, John Duncan, 1912
Interior photos and illustrations by Annwyn Avalon
Interior by Debby Dutton
Typeset in Adobe Jenson Pro, ITC Benguiat, and Frutiger LT Std

Printed in the United States of America
IBI
10 9 8 7 6 5 4 3 2 1

This book contains advice and information for using herbs and other botanicals, and is not meant
to diagnose, treat, or prescribe. It should be used to supplement, not replace, the advice of your
physician or other trained healthcare practitioner. If you know or suspect you have a medical
condition, are experiencing physical symptoms, or if you feel unwell, seek your physician's
advice before embarking on any medical program or treatment. Readers are cautioned to follow
instructions carefully and accurately for the best effect. Readers using the information in this
book do so entirely at their own risk, and the author and publisher accept no liability if adverse
effects are caused.

CONTENTS

ACKNOWLEDGMENTS

To my husband for showing me how a Goddess should
    be worshiped.
To my rose garden for always being there when I needed a break
    and for showing me the beauty of the Goddess within nature.
To my son for being so supportive and understanding.
To my Bestie for being the best.
To my mother for knowing I would be a writer before I did.
To Judika for giving me the opportunity and showing me the way.
To Anna for being the embodiment of the Earth Mother, and for
    churning the sacred waters with me always.

INTRODUCTION
Discovering the Goddess

Since I was a young girl, I have always yearned for the mysteries of life and understood that there was magic in nature. I spent my days collecting bugs, snakes, and swamp water in the solitude and soft embrace of the swampy mother goddess of nature. Although I was raised in a conservative Christian home, I knew deep within my bones that God is a woman, and that there is more than just one. As I reached puberty, I began drawing suns and moons. I drew them over and over, and gave them faces and personalities. Now, as a priestess, I understand the deep symbology here, and also chuckle when I look at my personal practice and how it surrounds the watery moon and solar goddesses.

While still in my pre-teen years, I was inspired to write a story about a girl who was a servant to Cleopatra. The story poured forth from me in a kind of madness, as if I were remembering something. I furiously typed the words on an old 1990s computer, spelling everything wrong and filling the pages with my infamous ten-line sentences. I remember this vividly, as if it happened yesterday. When I read the story, I didn't fantasize that I was Cleopatra; rather I felt as if I remembered seeing everything that happened to her. I think this may have been the moment when I remembered that God was much more than what I had read about in the Bible and that she was much more powerful and dynamic than what was found in those patriarchal pages

I named one of the characters in the story Aphrodite, a name that resonated in my head and I just couldn't shake it. A few years later, in high school, I chose her as the topic for an oral report. I dressed up in white and gold and carried my bowl of golden apples into class, proud of what I would talk about. I chuckle when I look back at this as well. Even before I really knew her, Aphrodite had me subtly proselytizing to a bunch of high-schoolers. Needless to say, I got an A+ on that assignment.

Not long after that, I began to joke around at the dinner table when my father made a big deal about holding hands and praying. When my father was done, he always finished with a resounding "Amen." Now, my father was the only man in the house—except for the cat—but I was the middle daughter of three. So I decided to add "and a couple of women." Later in life, I realized how potent and important this was. Not content to be just a bystander in my father's prayer, I was making it known that the Divine Feminine was not only present, but deserving of prayer, reverance, and worship, and no amount of indoctrination could erase what I believed or who I was. I was born to worship the Divine Feminine and serve at her feet. I was destined to become a priestess, even though I still had a lot of learning to do.

Around the same time, I spent several summer weeks in England, where I bought a few souvenirs and trinkets. One was a little plaster goddess statue that I packed carefully in my bags when I headed home. I have kept this with me over the years and, a few years later, this little statue played a huge role in a strange situation that kept me, a young nineteen-year-old, out of big trouble with the authorities. On seeing the statue and the strange shrine I had built to her, they understood that I was different and not just your average troublemaker. It wasn't until a few years later, when I was formally studying magic and witchcraft, that I understood who this goddess was and how she had always been with me—Sulis, my gracious mother, my protector, my guide.

I also bought two books on this trip that had a strange impact on my life. The truth is that, at that age, I had a complicated relationship with reading. I didn't like it; it was hard. My older sister spent all her time reading, always choosing to submerge herself in the thin pages of a book over spending time with her flesh-and-blood sister. As you can imagine, this made me quite resentful, so I teased her more than she probably deserved for reading all the time. The two books I bought were collections of Celtic fairy tales, stories from *The Mabinogi* and other tales inspired by Celtic folklore. And these books, like the little statue, have accompanied me as I have moved along the crooked path of my life.

Since my first encounter with Sulis, other goddesses have come into my life and acted as guides, lending help and healing, and sometimes administering a sharp swat to point me back on track. I hope that, in these pages, you experience your own magical encounters with the Celtic Divine Feminine, and that she reveals herself to you in powerful and moving ways.

When I was asked by my editor to write this book, I answered with an enthusiastic "yes!" I didn't hesitate. I knew this was a project I wanted to tackle. My own path to the Goddess had been a twisting journey of pain and hurt, but resulted in tranformation and healing beyond my imagination. If I could help others find her and make their paths a little easier, I would! I was excited to write about these divine women who have given and taught me so much.

As I began writing, however, parts of me froze. I wanted to write a scholarly book on goddesses—one that dove into the deepest depths of each divine being and shared her story with the world. But as I wrote, I found that the pressure of producing a perfect presentation of each goddess was simply not going to work. There was too little information about some of them and too much about others. Some had long stories and others were known only from a single inscription. How could I write something that would do each goddess justice? How could the words I would weave on the page begin to describe these magnificent beings adequately? How could I even include all the goddesses who are connected to the Celtic landscape?

To make matters worse, Celtic goddesses are usually not confined to one category. How could I organize this book in a way that made sense? Should I place Rhiannon under the section of mother goddesses, faery women, horse goddesses, or goddesses of magic? Is Cerridwen considered a lake lady, a mother goddess, or a faery woman? Should Sulis be placed under a section on healing or water? These divine beings are so dynamic; they take on so many powerful attributes and have so many layers to their stories, both in the historical record and in the context of their modern worship. I agonized over how I could create a book that was correct in every way— until I realized that I couldn't.

What I sought was a balance between creating an offering to the Celtic Ancestors, accurately describing the Celtic lands, and, most important, correctly portraying the Celtic goddesses who are so deeply woven into the tapestry of this tradition of magic and mystery. I wanted to build a bridge between the vastness of each goddess and those who seek her. In the end, I embarked on a goddess-guided journey, allowing them each to show me the highlights of their magic, and teach me what they wanted emphasized in the pages of this book—the best pathways for others to find them and experience their energy. The result is what I hope is an introduction to the many goddesses who belong to the Celtic lands and the people who worshiped them. I have done my best to give you tangible ways to meet these divine beings, understand them, and experience them for yourself. I do this through magic and folklore, as well as by explaining the ways in which they were honored and worshiped by our ancestors. Throughout these pages, I provide both traditional and modern exercises that are rooted in the cultural experiences of the British Isles to help you connect with each goddess.

To seek the Goddess is to seek the mysteries of nature, to yearn for the sacred embrace of the Mother, and to long to understand the mysteries of nature and of the self. It is a spiral path, leading you around and around, and back upon yourself. To seek the Goddess is to seek the depths of the earth and the soul of nature. We see her in the sky, in the waters, and in the landscape. We see nature shaping rocks in her image and trees embodying her energy. To seek her is to seek the lifeforce within—not just within ourselves but within nature, within the divine, and within the cosmic spiral of existence and the great mysteries of her power. To experience her firsthand, to be held in the arms of the healing Mother or to be dashed across the sea by the dark goddess and transformed into something greater than you were before. It often results in parts of you being stripped away, until your full and highest self is revealed.

Scholars have delved deep into the mythology, archaeology, and folklore of these sacred lands to understand who these divine beings were and what role they played in the lives of the Celts and those who now dwell within the Celtic landscape. I have spent countless hours reading these stories, pouring through archaeological data, and digging up obscure folklore. Through these studies, I have learned much about the Celtic Divine Feminine. But nothing has taught me more about these goddesses than encountering them myself through life, in ritual, and even by traversing the realms of the Otherworld through magic and shapeshifting. I hope that this book provides you with an opportunity to dip your toes in these magical waters and learn about these powerful, dynamic, and mysterious beings.

PART I

The Roots of Celtic Spirituality

CHAPTER 1

The Ancient Celts

There is no such thing as a single Celtic pantheon. Rather there are several groupings or families of goddesses and spirits found in ancient texts, along with archaeological evidence of the Divine Feminine scattered throughout Ireland, Scotland, England, Wales, Brittany, and other continental Celtic lands. When I began to write this book, I considered organizing it by region to emphasize the fact that there was no overarching lore or tradition of Celtic divinities, but rather goddesses and spirits specific to each of the sacred landscapes across the Celtic world.

I soon discovered, however, that this format failed to recognize that these divine beings were not, in many cases, restricted by boundaries imposed by humans. In fact, in both ancient and modern times, geographical and political boundaries have had little to do with the natural boundaries inherent within the Celtic landscape. Thus these goddesses must be seen through several lenses—from the perspective of the ancient Celts who worshiped them, through the cultural changes that have occurred over time, and in the context of modern devotees who are willing to experience them through ritual and dedication.

When you think of Celtic goddesses, your mind may immediately turn to the goddesses of Ireland. But Ireland is just a small fraction of the Celtic world. Celtic peoples once lived (and still do, to a lesser degree) throughout the British Isles—including in England, Ireland, Scotland, Wales, and the Isle of Man—and occupied large swaths of continental Europe, albeit in different places and at different times. Some of these Celts were known as Gauls, a tribal group that lived from the Iron Age well into the Roman period.

To complicate things further, the boundaries that defined the ancient Celtic tribes are completely different from the national boundaries we recognize today. The Roman invasion changed the face of Europe, as did the advent of Christianity and the subsequent rise and fall of kings. Thus the countries we know today as Ireland, England, Wales, Scotland, and France are irrelevant when researching Iron Age Celts. Moreover, there are large gaps in the historical record, as well as large gaps in the archaeological data, mythology, and folklore. Consequently, we can only do our best to piece together what we can to form a clear a picture of these traditions. For this book, the "Celts" will refer to the groups of peoples who at one time spoke Gaelic and the Brythonic languages in what is now Scotland, Ireland, Wales, Cornwall, England, France, Spain, and the Isle of Man.

Celtic Timeline:

Bronze Age, 3300–1200 BCE

Iron Age, 600 BCE–43 CE

Roman invasion of Britain, 43–400 CE

Mabinogi compiled in the 14th century CE

Medieval period, 5th to 15th century

Sadly, the Druids did not write anything down and left behind only an oral tradition. When this rich culture died out, so too did their ancient knowledge. To really understand who they were, we must examine the history of the landscape in which they lived and worshiped, including the archaeological record. We can also learn from the documentation left by the Romans, which most likely presents very biased accounts and so may not be completely trustworthy. We can search surviving medieval texts as well for clues about the nature of Celtic goddesses. One such text, *The Mabinogi*, compiled in the 14th century CE—long after the Iron Age—presents a biased Christian perspective that often portrayed women in a villainous light. In fact, the coming of the Christians left us with even less documentary evidence to go on. And, perhaps most significantly, we can look at the ancient traditions, folklore, and folk magic that have survived in the oral traditions of those who worshiped these goddesses. Central to these traditions is the power of the Divine Feminine.

THE DIVINE FEMININE

At the heart of the sacred Celtic landscape lies ancient knowledge of magical women, faery enchantresses, saints, sorceresses, and goddesses. But who were these enigmatic divine women? And how can we draw them into our everyday lives to experience their magic and mystery? The tradition contains fantastical stories of maidens who are eaten by dragons or are transformed into them. There are tales of magical women made from flowers, as well as of women who are fierce and warlike. The remnants of this folklore that have survived can teach us a lot about these divine beings—and also more about ourselves.

Celtic devotion to the Divine Feminine is complicated, to say the least. To understand it, you must accept that, in some cases, these goddesses will confuse you and remain far beyond your reach and comprehension. They cannot be put into neat little boxes or rigid categories. Their realms and descriptions overlap and are often contradictory and confusing. Brighid is one of the best examples this. She is worshiped and revered in a variety of ways throughout a wide range of landscapes and over a long span of time.

The Divine Feminine appears in many guises and forms within the Celtic world. In order to understand who these goddesses were, you must first understand the world the Celts inhabited and what it meant to be a Celt. The problem is that there are various interpretations of that world, and even those who identify as Celts today argue about what the word "Celtic" really means. There is much debate among scholars over who the Celts really were and who they are today, as well as over what can be identified as Celtic regions. In fact, in order to understand the Celtic world, we must first consider the various definitions and uses of the word.

The word "Celt," or *Keltoi*, was first used by the Greeks and first documented by the Romans in the 7th or 8th century BCE. The word itself was generally used to refer to a particular group of Indo-European peoples with cultural similarities who spoke related languages that were identified as Celtic in the ancient and medieval world. These tribes and cultures were dispersed over many countries and regions, and they developed distinct traditions that contained both many similarities and many differences.

The word "Celtic" is also used to describe a unique landscape. Thus, in order to truly understand the use of the word, we must delve into the literature and manuscripts left behind by these people, as well as study the modern culture of these regions and how it plays a part in various practices.

Some say that you must be born into a Celtic culture to be identified as a Celt. But that in itself is problematic, because, as we have seen, there is not one specific Celtic culture. Rather there are various tribes, regions, and countries that identify as Celtic. To make matters worse, throughout history, the word "Celtic" has been used to describe various peoples and locations, making it hard to pin down exactly who they were and where they lived. The Romans described the Celts in France, Belgium, and Germany as Gauls. But there were also other Celtic tribes who lived in what are now Portugal, Spain, Switzerland, and modern Turkey, although today the Turks are not Celtic and Turkey is not classified as a Celtic land.

When you first hear the phrase "Celtic lands," you probably immediately think of the British Isles. And, in fact, Wales, Ireland, Scotland, and England are all examples of Celtic lands that were inhabited by Celts (although not all who live there now are). Yet these regions all have unique cultures, languages, and folk customs. Likewise, Portugal, Spain, and France all have rich customs, folklore, and folk practices that can also be considered Celtic in nature or seen as descending from a Celtic tradition.

In the next chapter, we will explore what we know today as the Celtic world in order to better understand the role of the Divine Feminine in these rich traditions.

CHAPTER 2

The Celtic World

As we have seen, in order to really understand the Celtic goddesses and Celtic culture, we need to look at the nature of the Celts from different angles—from the perspective of the ancient Celts who worshiped them, through the cultural changes that time and modernity have wrought, and through the lens of devotees who are willing to experience them through ritual and dedication. We must consider the historical record, the archaeology, and cultural evidence that has survived in the landscape and the folklore. We also need to examine how various Celtic groups interacted with each other and how those practices have survived into the modern world. All of this taken together can shed light on the nature of Celtic traditions and thus give us insight into the divine women they worshiped.

The Romans played a large part in preserving and sometimes reshaping the Celtic and Gaulish goddesses. They not only brought their own deities into the lands they occupied; they also adopted and renamed many of the local goddesses. Coventina and Sulis are perfect examples of this. Coventina's shrine is located along the ruins of Hadrian's Wall, which was built by the Romans during their occupation of Britain. There is also evidence of her worship in Spain. In fact, it is widely believed today that Coventina may have been a Celtic goddess who was worshiped by Romans in the Celtic lands. Sulis, who is also known as Sulis Minerva, is another example of how the Romans adopted Celtic deities and preserved the knowledge of these powerful divine beings.

The descendants of the Celts and those who once lived in ancient Celtic lands are now scattered throughout Ireland, Scotland, Wales, Cornwall, Brittany, and some places in continental Europe, as well as across the world.

Moreover, the Celtic practices that originated in these regions have evolved and shifted, and been integrated into the practices of those who brought their own cultures with them as they conquered and explored distant lands. Research into similarities between the devotional practices of these integrated cultures can help us to deepen our knowledge of the the ancient Celts.

But it is also important to acknowledge and explore the differences between these cultures. For instance, although there are many similarities between the traditions of the Scots and the Irish, these two cultures remain very different in important ways. This is also true for the traditions of other Celtic lands. Although there are many overlaps and similarities, there are also clear distinctions. Thus it is hard to force the practices and goddesses of these various cultures into neat little boxes. Think of the Celts as being like a bowl of noodles—overlapping, intertwining, and interacting with each other while still remaining true to the evolution of their cultures.

THE ROLE OF WOMEN IN THE CELTIC WORLD

Celtic women were revered within their various societies; they weren't considered subservient or required to be obedient. They were pillars of strength who waged war on the Romans and they chose their own path. Prestigious positions in these societies were not reserved for men. Women held them as well and were able to own land and achieve status within their communities. Indeed, documentation indicates that, in early Celtic society, women could even pass their possessions and status down to their daughters. They fought in battle and, in the case of the British battle leader Boudica, led the fight against the Romans. Similarly, the Celtic queen Cartimandua led a group of Celtic tribes who were loyal to the Romans. Descriptions written by the Romans in letters back to Rome describe these women as terrifying and fierce. They also described Druids working in conjunction with priestesslike Celtic women who screamed incantations upon the wind as they fought the Roman invasion.

In order to really understand the mysteries of the goddesses of these lands, we must dive deep into the landscape. Many springs and waterways were sacred to the Celtic landscape and many goddesses were associated with springs, wells, and lakes. In some cases, they even share the name of the river with which they are linked. In other cases, goddesses were specifically thought to be the personification of the river itself. It was—and still is—widely believed that watery feminine spirits dwelled within each and every spring and well. Likewise, goddesses were often linked to and thought to dwell in sacred groves.

Celtic lands were invaded and occupied by many other cultures—the Anglo Saxons, the Romans, and the Vikings among them. These cultures generally sought to adopt and coexist with the local spirits of the land. But when Christians came to these sacred lands, they attempted to take control and drive the narrative. They co-opted worship at many of the sacred springs and rivers named for goddesses, and converted many sacred temples into churches. Many of the sacred wells once named for faery women, nymphs, and goddesses were renamed in honor of Christian saints. But the spirits never left these sacred places; they are still there—although, over time, they began to answer to different names.

The Roman and Christian occupations played a significant role in shaping the legacy of Celtic goddesses. When the Romans invaded a new land, they adopted, absorbed, and transformed the local deities, often renaming the deity who was worshiped at a particular place. Take Bath, for instance. Here, deep in the heart of Celtic lands, the Romans erected a huge temple complex to the Celtic goddess Sulis, adding the name of a Roman goddess, making her Sulis Minerva. This was unlike their usual practice. Most often, they changed the name of the deity completely or added the Roman name as a prefix—for example, Cunomaglus, a Celtic god associated with hounds whom the Romans renamed as Apollo Cunomaglus. But Bath was such an important sacred place to the local population that they adopted Sulis and gave her name precedence rather than co-opting her, thus helping to preserve her legacy. Another spring and well goddess who would have been lost to history and time if she had not been preserved and venerated by the Romans was Coventina, who was worshiped by both the Celts and the Romans. Her temple was located within the Roman settlement on Hadrian's Wall.

With the rise of Christianity, we see a similar thing happen, but with important differences. Churches were erected in sacred groves and near holy wells and, once again, the water nymphs who dwelled within the sacred springs were renamed. Faery springs became holy wells that were renamed for Christian saints. While some were renamed for male saints, which resulted in the complete loss of the original name associated with the goddess or feminine spirit, others retained their feminine associations and were renamed for female saints—like Brighid, who became conflated with Saint Brigit, and Anu, who became conflated with Saint Anne. What once was a Pagan sacred shrine became a source of holy water for a Christian church. Even the great Roman temple to Sulis lost its association with the Celtic goddess when a great abbey was erected directly on top of the ruins and dedicated to Saint Peter and Saint Paul. If it weren't for excavations done in the 18th century, which uncovered artifacts and inscriptions indicating that the original temple had been erected in honor of Sulis, we might never have known of its Celtic associations, and the healing waters would have continued to be linked with these male Christian saints.

To learn more about the adoption and co-opting of Celtic deities, we can turn to ancient texts and mythology that was written down. In general, Celtic traditions were oral traditions and, as these cultures disappeared or merged with invading cultures, most of the knowledge about them was lost. Fortunately, we have other means of learning about these goddesses. Ancient texts like the Welsh *Mabinogi*, the Irish Lebor *Gabála Érenn*, and medieval texts that describe goddesses like Melusine de Lusignan, although strongly influenced by Christianity, can still provide clues as to the true essence of these traditions. While Irish texts have similarities to those of the Welsh, there are very important differences within them, as there are between these cultures and their practices. The deities of Wales and those of Ireland are mostly distinct from one another, with a few particular overlaps and similarities. Though we will not be discussing this in detail, we will explore these stories in chapters to come. This is also true of the traditions and deities of Scotland and England, as well as of others.

Folk magical practices and folk stories have also been passed down from generation to generation. We even have a few texts from the medieval period relating magical and fantastical tales of joy, marriage, war, and grief. Although these were written with a Christian bias, we can still find clues in them that hint at their Pagan origins. Although some have been diminished to the status of fairy tales, the spirit of these stories has been preserved.

Although much of the Celtic tradition has been lost to us because of the lack of textual evidence, many of the ancient practices have been preserved in surviving folklore that has been handed down from generation to generation within families. This knowledge is vital to our understanding of the Celts, and especially of Celtic goddesses. It is quite possible, and honestly likely, that these practices have been altered and changed over time, but it still remains true that they originated within the Celtic landscape and are true reflections of Celtic culture. Although modern folk practices may not be performed in exactly the same way they were during the Iron Age, they are still rooted in the lives of the people who dwelled in Celtic lands.

In the chapters to come, we will explore Celtic goddesses from these various perspectives, and dive deep into the heart of the Celtic landscape. We'll learn stories passed down across time, and look at the archaeological record and at invading cultures. We'll examine goddesses who are considered to be Celtic, as well as others who may not have been of Celtic origin, but were venerated nonetheless within Celtic traditions and in Celtic lands—like Coventina. We'll also turn to old texts, remnants of history, and folklore to find the true nature and deep meaning of what and who these Celtic goddesses were.

To begin, let's learn a little about the Celtic Otherworld.

CHAPTER 3

The Celtic Otherworld

There is no underworld in the Celtic tradition; rather there is an Otherworld that consists of three realms—land, sea, and sky. This Otherworld is quite paradoxical in nature. It is a place of magic, mystery, and transformation that consists of liminal places and is inhabited by liminal beings. It is often associated with the dead, but at the same time is full of life and the living. It should not be confused with other cultural renderings of the underworld or the afterlife. Although some references state or hint at it being a place where we go when we die, some also indicate it is a place from which we may return. Beings from the Otherworld are often said to be able to travel to this world with ease, and stories of children, midwives, and heroes who are stolen away to the Otherworld and return years later are common.

It is also important to note that the passage of time, the rules of human society, and the laws of physics do not operate in the same way in the Celtic Otherworld as they do in this world. Some stories indicate that the Otherworld is a subaquatic village that can be accessed through various portals. In other cases, it is variously described as a liminal shoreline or a mysterious island that is located either in the west or across the depths of the ocean. It may lay shrouded in a thick gray mist, beyond a river, across a hedge, or down a well. Others indicate that, during liminal times of the year, this world and the Otherworld become one.

The three realms of the Otherworld are often represented by modern practitioners by an ancient symbol called the "triskele," a triple spiral that can help us understand the mysteries of the Celtic goddesses (see Figure 1). This symbol represents the dynamic symmetry that exists within the three realms. But the land, the sea, and the sky of the Celtic Otherworld are not analogous to the elements of earth, water, and air in other traditions, and should not be confused with them. The elements exist within these realms, but they are not themselves the elements. These mythological spaces are both separate from and the same as the physical world. At certain times of the year, the veil between these two worlds lifts and they become one.

Figure 1. Triskele, a triple spiral that can represent the three realms of the Celtic Otherworld.

The three realms of the Otherworld are associated by modern practitioners with the colors red, black, and white, colors that we find throughout Celtic mythology and folklore. The mythic animals that populate this world often appear in these colors. The Cwn Annwn—the "Hell Hounds" of the faery king Gwyn ap Nudd—are white with red eyes and red-tipped ears. The white horse and white stag are both symbols of Otherworldly magic. Black dogs often appear in folklore as liminal omens of death, while boars and pigs, especially white ones, are seen as coming from the Otherworld. Magical and sacred cows play a role as well. Cows are sacred to goddesses like Brighid, and magical cows rise out of the lake in the story of the Lady of Llyn y Fan Fach. Irish tales tell of three sacred cows—one black, one red, one white—named Bo-Dhu, Bo Ruadh, and Bo-Finn.

The legends of Avalon tell us that it was once named Ynys Afallach, which means "Isle of Afallach." Afallach was a Welsh king whose name derives from *afal*, which means "apple." The apple is a fruit that contains all three of these colors—black seeds, white meat, and red skin. We can also see these three realms reflected in the story of Cerridwen when she chases little Gwion Bach through them, shapeshifting into a land animal, then a creature of the water, and finally into a creature of the air. This is also true of Melusine, who is portrayed as both a water serpent or mermaid and as a faery woman and fertility goddess connected to earth. Ultimately, she takes to the sky and flies to a mountain, thus traveling through the realm of air.

Cauldrons feature prominently in Celtic lore as well—especially in Welsh and Irish mythology—and still play an important role in the craft of witches today. These are sacred vessels, crucibles for magic, and representations of the sacred Mother. Cerridwen's cauldron brews three drops of Awen; Dagda's cauldron, the *coire ansic*, is perpetually filled; and the Nine Maidens of Annwn kindle the Cauldron of Rebirth.

But cauldrons are not the only sacred vessels found in Celtic lore. There are silver bowls that help create thunderstorms and enchantments, as described in Chrétien de Troyes' *Lady of the Fountain*, and golden bowls used by well maidens, like those found in the *Elucidation*, as well as the silver bowl or cauldron found in Rhiannon's story. The chalice of the holy grail is another symbolic cauldron, as is the bronze bowl found in the archaeological excavations of the Celtic Lake Village in Glastonbury. This bowl, one of the many Iron Age artifacts found there, has large nodules surrounding the basin for decoration. These cauldron-like vessels have a deep significance to Celts that goes far beyond just cooking and washing.

WATERY WOMEN

The Otherworldly realm of water holds special power and meaning in Celtic tradition because it connects with the ancestral realms and the realms of the water spirits. Moreover, the link between water and women in the Celtic world is deep and mysterious. Sacred sites connected with rivers and sacred wells were named for goddesses called "tutelary deities," who were revered as protectors and guardians of particular places. The role of tutelary goddesses also brings in the concept of guardianship and protection. These beings were described as both goddesses and nature spirits, and some were associated with specific individuals. In fact, the term may describe a deity or nature spirit who is associated with an individual from first breath to last—a being who is sometimes considered to be a "familiar."

Water was thought to be sacred across the Celtic world. We know this from the survival of devotional offerings made to lakes, rivers, wells, and springs, as well as from the numerous shrines and ritual sites that have been found at locations associated with water. The Celts saw water as a portal to the Otherworld. Stories of lake maidens who lived in villages hidden under the water's surface are commonplace in Celtic lore. Offerings were often thrown into lakes or wells to transport them from this world to the land of the Ancestors or to the Otherworld as offerings in exchange for favor, healing, and sometimes cursing. From surviving artifacts, we know that offerings deposited into these sacred places were often broken before they were placed into the water. This created a "death-like" state for the object before it was sent into the Otherworld. In some cases, bodies of water like lakes and wells were seen as portals; in other cases, the water itself was seen as part of the Otherworld.

Despite the Roman invasion and occupation, these watery sites remained sacred to the local people, and the Romans, instead of destroying them and their goddesses, just renamed them, often adding the names of their own goddesses to the names of the Celtic deities. This happened in the case of Sulis Minerva, Brighid, and others.

Even after the fall of the Roman Empire and the subsequent rise of Christianity, the local Celts continued to love, worship, and honor their goddesses and spirits at these sacred sites. The Christian Church, in a kind of forced conversion, simply reconsecrated them as churches and shrines, often changing the names of the local goddesses or spirits to the names of predominantly female saints, who became the guardians of the springs and wells. Nonetheless, despite the change in name and rulership, the worship didn't cease. Nor did the belief of the local population that the traditional goddesses and spirits still dwelled in those sacred places. In fact, they never left their watery homes; they were just called by different names to reflect the spirituality of the current dominant religion.

MAGICAL BEASTS

Magical beasts also play a large role in the Celtic Otherworld, and are thus crucial to an understanding of the Celtic Divine Feminine and Celtic spirits and goddesses. Celtic goddesses were often associated with or portrayed as bird-women, and faery-like beings or winged creatures are found throughout Celtic mythology. Melusine transforms into a winged dragon; Rhiannon is renowned for her magical birds. Morgan le Fae is described as having wings that she can take on or off, like those of Daedalus. Blodeuwedd is changed from an Otherworldly flower maiden into an owl as part of her punishment for infidelity, lending a shapeshifting aspect to this enigmatic figure.

Crows, swans, and other aquatic birds are prominent features in the Celtic Otherworld. In the story of the swan maiden, a young girl either shapeshifts into a swan or is turned into one against her will. Cerridwen shapeshifts into a bird as a result of her anger and frustration in her pursuit of young Gwion Bach. The Morrigan is associated with both battle crows and ravens. And this image of faery women or women with wings resonates with the Christian portrayal of winged angels, giving us yet another indication that these women were Otherworldly or divine in some way.

Boars and pigs were also common beasts in the Otherworld, and some goddesses were described as riding on boars. Others, like Melusine and Henwen, are associated with these beasts, which increase their connection to the Otherworld or augment their magical powers of divination. Deer maiden are also common in depictions of the Otherworld, often lurking quietly on the corner of a page in ancient texts or recalling a distant memory, as are horse goddesses like Rhiannon, Epona, and Macha.

MAGICAL WOMEN

The common theme that runs through all these descriptions of the Celtic Otherworld is the central role of women. So what makes Celtic women so powerful within this tradition? Celtic women were fierce, and this is reflected in warrior goddesses like Andraste and The Morrigan. Although there were clearly differences across the role of women in different Celtic regions, in almost all these traditions, women were figures of power. And this power is reflected in the prominence of the Divine Feminine in Celtic lore and mythology. Despite regional differences, Celtic goddesses all share characteristics like sovereignty, liminality, an association with the three realms of the Otherworld, skill with magical herbs, and the use of sacred vessels with magical powers.

When considering these mysterious magical women, we must take into account archaeology, mythology, and folklore. The information we have about the many goddesses that were worshiped in Celtic lands comes from

Figure 2. Relief of Brighid with a cow, indicating her connection to cattle and livestock.

these three sources. Some goddesses—like Sulis, the Matres, and Epona—survive only in the archaeological record. Artifacts, temple remnants, and statues are the only evidence we have of their presence in the lives of the Celts. In the case of Irish and Welsh goddesses, we have ancient texts. The Arthurian romances give us a deeper insight into these goddesses and the various layers of their stories. And because Celtic goddesses are deeply connected to the landscape, the landscape itself can also be viewed as having its own story to tell that can reveal clues to deities about whom we have very little information. We should not neglect this resource. Moreover, some goddesses still survive deep within the hearts of the Celts and their descendants, their stories having been passed down from mother to daughter over time, until they were eventually recorded in books of folklore.

Myth and magic surround these diverse magical women. These beings could shapeshift, heal, create, regenerate, and wage war. It is important to note that Celtic goddesses do not fit neatly into the modern archetypes of maiden, mother, and crone. Some seem to manifest as more than one of these archetypes, and others wield powers that do not correspond to any of those archetypes at all! Some goddesses and nymphs appear in groups of three—like The Morrigan and the Matronae—but not as the modern construct of a triple goddess. Rather they are seen as "triune" or "triformis," or may represent different aspects of the same goddess who shapeshifts into different forms or exhibits different attributes. Melusine, for instance, can appear as a faery woman, a mermaid, or a dragon, while Sulis can be seen as a goddess of healing, of curses, or of liminality. Celtic lore also contains examples of groups of nine women. Some are priestesses, like the nine priestesses of Avalon, the nine priestesses of the Isle of Sena, and the nine sisters who were devoured by a dragon in Scotland. Others are considered to be magical maidens, like the Korrigan or the Nine Maidens of Annwn.

In the midst of all this diversity, there is at least one goddess who can be found throughout most of the Celtic world—although there are variations on her name and differences in her nature—and this is Brighid, who appears as both a goddess and a saint (or both), and plays a role in many diverse folk traditions and practices.

Each of these magical women represents a dynamic force that cannot really be reduced to an archetype. They are more than just archetypes. They are individual divine beings with rich stories and layered feelings. We'll explore these mysterious divine beings in the chapters to come.

CHAPTER 4

Celtic Rituals and Devotional Practices

The magic of the Celtic tradition goes deeper than the first recorded writing of the stories of their goddesses and the archaeological evidence we have uncovered so far. These can only provide snapshots of times gone by—past perceptions of these sacred beings and the Divine Feminine that can only inform our understanding and practice in the way that a photograph conveys an actual subject. We can try to piece these past perceptions together, but our understanding of them still remains partial and fragmented.

In fact, Celtic-inspired rituals and devotional practices are so varied that each person's experience of them is unique. Moreover, each personal experience will differ from the experience before. It is up to us to draw close to the lore of each goddess and get to know the cultures that originally worshiped her. In your personal practice, it is important to lean on the past to inform the present and to understand the cultural context of each goddess and those originally devoted to her. Understanding how Scottish, Irish, English, and French women lived through different times and how they honored the Divine Feminine can help you understand each goddess on a level that goes deeper than superficial research or the information given in this book.

In the chapters to come, I provide a portrait of these goddesses, as well as exercises that can help you get to know them. But this is just a starting point—a ticket to ride on your quest to understand the cosmic energies of these beings. Here, we will examine the best way to begin working with these goddesses, how to listen to and forge a relationship with them, how to develop devotional practices, how to establish reciprocity with the divine, and how to give offerings. We'll also explore color associations for each goddess, as well as suggested herbs and crystals, and traditional crafts. And

I'll teach you how to perform devotional rituals and how to honor these divine women by building altars and shrines. To help you better understand your experience, I provide journal questions that can help you reach out to the dynamic and mysterious nature of these enigmatic beings.

ENCOUNTERING THE GODDESSES

There are many ways to encounter Celtic goddesses. I have experienced them in many different ways and in many different guises. I have had them quietly guide and protect me, without even knowing what was happening until much later. I have had them follow me quietly; I have had them ask to be acknowledged when I ignored their call. I have selfishly chased after others and been left feeling empty. I have slowly and patiently honored them without want or need or expectations. And I have formed life-long relationships with amazing magical beings who have shown me the mysteries of death and life, changed me, held me, and healed me. I have also collided with others who left me shocked and feeling depleted and torn apart, only then to be stitched back together, transformed and renewed. No matter how you first encounter a goddess—through love and healing, or through grief and destruction—the key is to form a relationship of reciprocity that is honorable. This is how you deepen your relationship with the goddess and the things she represents and brings into your life.

When you begin to seek out or work with a goddess, there are a few things to keep in mind. If you have been influenced or indoctrinated by very structured or fundamentalist types of religion, you may have certain ideas about what it means to worship a deity. Authoritarian religions often promote practices based in petitioning and supplication, placing great emphasis on unworthiness and the need to repent. When working with Celtic goddesses, this is generally not the case, although there are some exceptions.

Don't get me wrong. There have been times when I found myself on my knees before the altar of a goddess in a humbled and reverent attitude. But I have never had a goddess demand this of me or hold lofty threats over my head for lack of devotion, worship, or faith. When a goddess appears in your life, rest assured that nothing like this will ever be demanded of you. What you can expect from working with most goddesses is guidance and a deep relationship with the self and with nature. What you can expect is an invitation to healing and transformation—and, when needed, a swift kick in the right direction.

When you form a relationship with a goddess, it is important to understand that it must be reciprocal in nature. This means that you build a relationship formed around devotional acts like creating an altar, meditation, prayer, incantations, singing, and reading or writing poetry. You reach out by performing rituals to honor the goddess and fulfilling tasks that are asked of you. These can often be actions to benefit the environment, to better yourself, to push past your own limitations, or to explore the mysteries of magic.

A relationship with a goddess can last a lifetime and is not something that should be rushed. Each goddess—no matter how much or how little of her story is supported by mythology, archaeology, or modern worship—is deeply layered and dynamic. Here, I hope to give you an introduction to the magic of these beings, which can take a lifetime to explore. Each goddess presented here has her own lesson to teach, and sometimes these lessons are harsh. But sometimes they are lessons of healing that can be quite beautiful or leave you feeling rung out and raw.

When a goddess first appears to you, you may have very diverse experiences depending on the one with whom you are working. Some may appear to you as beautiful maidens, while others may be Otherworldly phantoms that leave you shaken. But sometimes fear is useful, because it tells us to be aware and to pay attention. Sometimes fear can help us to break through blocks or discover where we need healing. And sometimes that is exactly the message a goddess wants to convey. The key is to be silent and to listen, for the goddesses often speak in the silence and in the liminal spaces.

Begin by performing little devotional acts like building an altar or shrine to the goddess with whom you want to work. Spend time at her sacred sites; research her mythology; write poetry, prayers, and incantations that honor her; perform singing and dancing rituals to reach out to her.

Remember as you work with Celtic goddesses—or with any spirit, for that matter—that they are not magical resources that you can draw on at will. They are living entities, divine beings and spirits deeply connected with the earth. They may not be happy to receive demands or requests from strangers any more than you would be happy to find ten strangers at your front door on a Saturday night asking for money, or food, or help. Approach these divine spirits as the goddesses they are—beings worthy of your respect and honor.

CHOOSING A GODDESS

I recommend not trying to "choose a goddess" based on what is trendy or what your friends or those in your magical circle are doing. Although this is sometimes successful, it can often result in failure, because your intentions are not pure. Instead, allow a goddess (or goddesses) to choose you. Or choose one to whom you feel an emotional connection so that you can establish a relationship that goes beyond the superficial.

Each person's relationship with a goddess will be different, regardless of whether you choose her or she chooses you. Because every situation will be different, each relationship will be as layered and perplexing as the mysterious goddesses you seek. You may set out to forge a relationship with one goddess and find only silence. You may find that you are drawn to just one goddess or to many goddesses. Or you may establish a relationship with one goddess, only to have another come knocking at your door. You may even find that many come knocking and that you are overwhelmed.

In her book *The Essential Guide to Possession, Depossession, and Divine Relationships*, Pagan priestess and scholar Diana L. Paxson calls this "being god bothered." If this happens to you, please contact your local witch, Pagan or metaphysical shop, local grove, or community circle to find a mentor who can guide you on the spirit-working path. These can be tricky and tumultuous waters, and having a guide who has navigated them before is important.

Spirits of the sacred feminine are not one-dimensional and are far more elaborate than can be understood from the smattering of history, folklore, mythology, and archaeology we have available to us. They, like humanity, have evolved over time. If you really want to know these spirits, study, read, research, and learn as much about them as you can from the sources we have. But remember that these sources provide only snapshots of the true nature of these beings and the people who revered them. A better question to ask is: Who is this goddess to me?

To discover this, you can turn to what is known as "unverified personal gnosis," or UPG. UPG usually comes from direct contact with a spirit. It provides information that sometimes can not be verified in any way and that may not necessarily align with what is recorded in history. What you learn through UPG may either differ from or align with information provided by verified sources. In short, it is the information you get from working with and listening to a spirit, which can sometimes be difficult to understand or confusing because direct communication with spirits can come in a variety of ways. Sometimes the goddesses speak in riddles and rhymes; sometimes they speak in symbols and stories; sometimes they speak through signs and omens. My own experience of these beings has been a combination of clear speech, symbology, and signs. The key is to listen and to learn whatever magic is there to be discovered.

This kind of direct communication provides insights that can vary from practitioner to practitioner, and that may depend on the psychic skills you have naturally or have developed. And the truth is that everyone can experience spirit contact, even if they don't think they have psychic skills. These skills can be developed with patience and practice. If you are interested in learning more about developing these skills, contact your local occult shop and see if they have classes or can recommend a local teacher. They may also carry books that can help you in your quest.

The rest of this chapter will be devoted to exercises and practices that can help you reach out to the goddesses in a number of ways and learn to incorporate that contact into your daily life.

Exercise: Seeking Wisdom in the Standing Stones

This Immram is inspired by the standing stones of Stenness in Orkney. An Immram is much like a visualization or meditation. It is an old Irish way of describing a journey to the Otherworld, most often over water. In this book, it will be used to describe vision journeys, meditations, and visualizations that are meant to take you on your own hero's journey through the mist or across the hedge and into the Celtic Otherworld. In this Immram, you'll travel to the magical isle of Orkney, where you will encounter a number of Celtic goddesses and gain wisdom from and knowledge of the Otherworld. Even if you already work with a Celtic goddess, this meditation can open the door to the magical possibilities of forging a relationship with divine beings. Perhaps the same goddess will come to you in a different guise or with a different message, helping you to uncover more of the mysteries and magic of the Celtic Otherworld.

For this exercise, you will need a journal and a pen or pencil. Keep this right beside you so that, as soon as you leave your meditative state, you can write down everything that you have seen, heard, and felt. Be sure to note any feelings, symbols, colors, clothing, hairstyles, companions, images, and plants that appeared in the background. This information can help you discover which goddess you are encountering. If you have trouble with visualization or memorizing, open a recording program on your computer or phone and read this aloud. You can then play it back as a guided meditation.

To begin, find a comfortable position, either seated or lying down. Soften your mind, close your eyes, and allow yourself to relax. Take nine long slow breaths. As you do this, let your body relax, clear your mind, and release the stress of the day. This time, this moment right now, is for you. Just relax and focus on your breathing.

In your mind's eye, focus on darkness and allow your mind to go quiet. As you explore this darkness, see a small sliver of light begin to move toward you. It grows larger and larger, moving upward until you can start to make out a silver disk in the sky. It illuminates your surroundings and you find yourself on the sandy shores of a beach. You walk the shore, the liminal place between sea and land, until you come across a curious small round vessel called a coracle. This vessel floats in the water, inviting you to climb in.

As you board the wobbly vessel, you notice the fine details of sacred symbols carved into its structure. You take the paddle and begin to navigate the crashing waves, sailing over one, two, three, four, five, six, seven, eight, nine. As you crest the ninth wave, you enter into the unknown watery realms of the Otherworld. You now travel upon the water with ease, gliding past sharp cliffs, rocky shores, and sandy beaches. You glide away from the mainland toward a cluster of islands. As if you are no longer steering the coracle, it whisks you through the water and pulls you toward one island in particular.

When you arrive on shore, you climb out of your boat and walk toward the center of the island, where you see three tall stones with long straight edges and sharp angles. This is the stone circle of Stenness, one of the oldest Neolithic sites in the British Isles. Long before the Celts and others arrived here, these stones stood watching over these magical shores. They hold within them the wisdom of tide and time. They are the great observers that stand sentinel over the mysteries of the land. They have guarded these mysteries for thousands of years, collecting and recording both magical and mundane knowledge across the march of time. Now you seek their wisdom.

As you walk slowly through these tall stones, you see a smaller grouping of stones off to the side. You turn and walk toward them. You see three stones in a strange formation and a large rectangular stone lying flat against the earth that looks like a crude stone altar. Behind it are two upright stones that are curved and worn on the outside edges, but sharp and flat in the center, as if they were once one stone that was snapped cleanly down the center. Together, they look almost like a doorway or portal that is too small to step through. As you gaze at this strange formation, you notice that the stones are covered in strange interwoven carvings.

You step up to the stone altar and peer down at it, noticing a deep crevice in the center that is full of water. As you peer into this little pool of water, you see it begin to vibrate. You kneel down to get a closer look, and the water begins to ripple and swirl, forming a spiral. You watch the beauty and rhythm of it. The spiral begins to speed up, until you can barely make it out. The water clears for a just moment and in it you see a vision of a woman. This vision separates into three parts, each curling outward and all spiraling in the same direction. The vision takes the shape of a triskele. You continue to gaze at the symbol as you wait for the feminine vision to reappear.

Once again, the water moves and shifts and the woman appears in it. Take time to observe her; look at her hair, her eyes, her clothes. Notice what is behind her and what she carries with her. Be sure to pay attention to where she is and what type of adornment she wears. If you wish to commune with her, you can pause and take time here to speak and listen.

Soon, your time with her comes to an end and the image begins to fade and the rapid swirling appears in the water once again, gradually slowing until it turns to just a ripple, then just a shimmer, then finally settles into stillness.

You stand up, dust off your knees, and head back to the vessel waiting for you on the shore. It swiftly takes you back in the direction you came, passing by each of the beaches and rocky cliffs you passed before, until you reach the place from which you started. You leave the vessel and walk back across the sandy beach. Taking a deep breath, you gaze up into the night sky, which is illuminated by the moon. You gaze at the moon and notice that it looks brighter and feels closer than it did before. As you gaze at it, it grows and brightens, until you are blinded by its silvery white light. The brilliance of the light forces you to close your eyes and you find youself in complete darkness once again.

Begin to focus on your physical breath, feeling the air come in and out of your lungs, sensing it as it passes through your nose. Bring your attention to your hands and feet. Begin to wiggle your fingers and toes, moving gently up to your wrist and ankles. Then gently move your head from side to side. Take one more deep breath and come back into this time and this space.

While this experience is still fresh in your mind, record your impressions in your journal. What symbols were on the stones? In which direction did the water swirl? Clockwise, or sunwise, may indicate that the goddess you encountered is associated with the upper realms as well as the solar realms. Counterclockwise, or countersunwise, may indicate a goddess associated with nocturnal realms, the ancestral realms, or death. What age did the goddess you encountered appear to be? What did she look like? What was she holding? Where was she?

Record these impressions in your journal so that you can return to them later and consider their significance.

Exercise: Building an Altar or Sacred Space

When you are building altars to specific goddesses, it is important to focus on the preferences and sacred associations of each goddess. In Part II, you will find these sacred associations and attributes listed at the beginning of each chapter. I have drawn these directly from mythology, folklore, and the archaeological record. In some cases, I also give associations drawn from modern Pagan worship, from practicing devotees, and even from pop culture. Use the information in these lists to make appropriate choices as you design and construct your altar.

Some spirits prefer to keep their altars and shrines secret from the prying eyes of the world. Others are not as picky and may even encourage sharing. You can meditate and use your intuition to discover the preference of the goddess you are honoring. You can also allow the goddess to speak through the simple divination practice of tossing a coin. If in doubt, keep your altar private until you are confident about what your chosen goddess prefers.

To begin, find a flat space that is away from little fingers, fluffy paws, and the eyes of curious guests. Consider whether you are creating a public shrine in a magical space where you offer devotion to the goddess or practice magic. In this case, although it may be tended by you, it may be used by others, so make sure that you place it somewhere accessible. To open a relationship with a goddess, I suggest starting with a personal altar where you can feel free to express yourself and communicate with her in the way that is best for you—a place where you won't feel judged by anyone.

Be sure to have a design or a plan in mind for your altar. Will you put candles on it? If the goddess you seek has any solar or fire associations, be sure to add some. If this is the case, a bookshelf may not be the best place to set your altar. If you are reaching out to a water goddess whose shrine will hold only water, however, you can place it in a space like a bookshelf without fear of damaging the shelf or risking a fire.

Next, decide whether or not you want to use an altar cloth. Although these can be really beautiful and I love to use them, they are not practical for me because I tend to be very messy when I work, so wax, water, ash, and plant debris often ruin the cloth. For this reason, I generally only use altar cloths in ritual settings and keep my shrines and altars fabric-free, although in recent years I have enjoyed using doilies to decorate them.

In the next three exercises, you'll learn how to create and bless three other important elements of a sacred altar—a sacred image, sacred candles, and a sacred vessel.

Exercise: Consecrating, Dedicating, and Anointing a Sacred Image

As you design your altar or shrine, be sure to include a sacred image, effigy, or statue that can represent the goddess you seek. First choose a statue or image of the goddess that resonates with you. Gather together spring water, holy water, or another magical water blend found later in this book, as well as salt or sacred earth and a bundle of herbs to burn. I suggest using rosemary, mugwort, lavender, juniper, or other evergreens for this. Be sure you have these ready and use them as described below.

Sprinkle the water on the figure you want to consecrate, while saying:

I consecrate this figure with sacred waters of this earth.

Light the bundle of herbs and pass the figure through the smoke, or spiral the smoke bundle from the feet to the head, going around the body in a sunwise direction, while saying:

I consecrate this figure with sacred smoke from this earth.

Sprinkle salt or sacred earth on the figure, while saying:

I consecrate this figure with sacred salt created upon this earth.

You can also place the figure in the center of three candles and light them as you say this, but replace the word "salt" with "fire."

Finally, speak this blessing over the figure you are consecrating:

I consecrate this figure in the name of _____ (the goddess you have chosen or who has chosen you). I dedicate this figure, shaped in the likeness of my beloved goddess to the powers of love.

I dedicate this figure, the physical representation of my divine goddess to be the object of my devotion.

I dedicate this figure in the name of _____ (the goddess you have chosen or who has chosen you), she who is powerful, she who is magic, she who is my beloved.

Once the statue or image is consecrated and blessed, place it in an appropriate place on your altar.

Exercise: Anointing, Dressing, and Blessing Sacred Candles

Candles are particularly important for altars built to goddesses with sacred associations with fire and the sun. They can also add a richness and power to rituals performed on altars built to other deities and spirits. It is important when choosing and dressing your candles to pay attention to the preferences and associations of the goddess you have chosen to worship.

First, create an herbal blend. Here is a lovely blend you can begin with. Place rose petals, lavender, rosemary, mugwort, hawthorn flowers, elder flowers, mugwort, juniper, and queen of the meadow in a mortar and grind them into a fine powder with a pestle. Then choose the oil you want to use—perhaps rosemary, rose, or lavender, but any plant-based oil will do. Finally, choose your candle color according to the modern magical color associations listed for your goddess:

- Red for associations with love, passion, blood, fire, empowerment, strength, and ferocity
- Blue for associations with healing, water, and emotions
- Green for associations with abundance, fertility, money, the green world, and growth
- Yellow for associations with solar energies, friendship, warmth, light, and happiness

- Orange for associations with solar energies, chaos, and energy
- Purple for associations with royalty, divinity, comfort, and authority
- White for associations with purity, new beginnings, cleansing, purification, and rebirth
- Black for associations with protection, banishment, dark goddesses, the New Moon, nocturnal energies, death, transformation, and binding
- Gray for associations with depression, twilight, liminality, and the in-between
- Silver for associations with the moon, battle, defense, reflection, and shields
- Gold for associations with solar energies, money, and royalty

Once you have chosen the appropriate colors for your candles, you are ready to dress and bless them.

For general anointing, start in the middle of the candle. Dip your fingers in the oil and move them slowly toward the top of the candle, saying:

> With this sacred oil I anoint this candle.

Then dip your fingers back in the consecrated liquid and, starting in the middle of the candle, move them slowly toward the base of the candle, saying:

> With this sacred oil I anoint this candle.

If you are anointing for manifestation, use these same steps, but begin with your fingers at the tip of the candle and move them directly toward you, as if you are bringing something to you. If you are anointing for banishment, use the same steps, but begin with your fingers at the base of the candle and move them directly away from you, as if you were pushing something away from you.

Finally, take the ground herbal blend and sprinkle it onto the oily candle. You can also choose to roll the candle in the herbs to give it a generous coating. As you do this, say:

> With the power of these nine magical herbs I sprinkle their virtues
> upon this candle.

You can modify this ritual using various plants and blends suggested throughout the book to prepare candles for your various needs.

Exercise: Finding and Consecrating a Sacred Vessel

Sacred vessels can be of a variety of shapes and styles, although sacred bowls and chalices are most common. Bowls are perhaps a bit more practical, as they can be great places to put offerings, pour liquids, cast spells, and scry for visions, but chalices are popular as well. I personally have many sacred bowls and a few sacred chalices. You can even use baskets and other types of containers, like pitchers, teapots, and cups. And remember that cauldrons are also used as sacred vessels. Several of the exercises that follow use cauldrons, and you may wish to go through a consecration ritual like this before using them.

You can consecrate a sacred vessel for a particular purpose, or you can dedicate it to a particular goddess or practice, like scrying. In this exercise, we will focus on finding one vessel and doing a basic consecration. You can then use these steps as a guide for future consecrations and eventually develop your own style by adding your own flourishes.

It is also important to note that sacred vessels may not last forever and it is useful to keep a working collection of them in case one breaks in the middle of a ritual. If this happens, remove it immediately, cleanse the area, and bury the pieces near your outdoor altar. If you don't have an outdoor altar, or you feel that malevolence was involved in the breaking of the vessel, take it to the nearest crossroads or other liminal location and dispose of it there. After you do, be sure to turn around immediately and don't look back. Once the vessel has been placed into the hands of spirit, you don't need to know more. Taking it to the dump or placing it in the trash is also appropriate, especially if it is not biodegradable or you are concerned about littering.

And remember that breaking an object before giving it as an offering was a common practice in the ancient world. The breaking of the object made it useless in the physical world and it suffered a symbolic death and entered the Otherworld.

When choosing your sacred vessel, first consider what you have on hand. You may already have beautiful chalices or bowls that you never use. Consider using these first. If you don't have anything appropriate, you can use family heirlooms and connect to your ancestral lineage. If you still haven't found the right vessel, head to your local metaphysical shop or an art festival and see what you can find. You can also use second-hand items found at vintage shops and estate sales. No matter what you choose, be sure it feels right for you. And try to choose something that isn't too fragile and that fits conveniently on your altar.

To consecrate a sacred vessel, you use the energies of land, sea, and sky. Use salt to invoke the energies of the land, sacred or holy water to invoke the energies of the sea, and incense to invoke the energies of the sky. You can then make slight adjustments using the correspondences given at the head of each chapter to personalize the vessel for the goddess of your choice. For example, if you want to consecrate a vessel to Sulis or another solar goddess, dry calendula or sunflower petals, grind them into a powder, and add them to the salt to tint it yellow. Or you can create an incense from calendula petals, chamomile, frankincense, and cedar to add solar energies. You can also make a solar water by placing water in a vessel and charging it in the sun with a few chamomile flowers floating in it.

To begin, prepare your chosen salt, water, and incense blends. Once they are ready, place all three on the edges of your altar, leaving space in the center for the unconsecrated vessel. First, sprinkle the salt blend all over the bowl. Pick it up, turn it around, and sprinkle the salt everywhere. (Yes, this can be a bit messy.) As you do so, say:

> With this salt, I cleanse this vessel. May the powers of the sacred earth be consecrated upon this sacred vessel.

Then dust off the salt and place the bowl back on the altar.

Next, pour just a tiny amount of the water blend you have prepared into the center of the bowl. Use your hands to begin washing the bowl, covering every inch of it, inside and out, with the water. As you do this, say:

> With this water, I cleanse this vessel. May the powers of the sacred waters be consecrated upon this sacred vessel.

Then pass the vessel through the smoke from your incense blend. Be sure to turn and twist it so that every inch of the vessel is touched by the smoke. If the vessel is a chalice or cauldron, hold it upside down and allow it to fill with smoke. While you do this, say:

> With this smoke, I cleanse this vessel. May the powers of the sacred air be consecrated upon this sacred vessel.

When you are finished, place the consecrated vessel back in the center of your altar. It is ready to be used in magic and ritual!

Exercise: Celtic Goddess Simmer Pot

Here is a simple formula for a simmering pot of herbs that you can use to add a scent to your home or your altar space that will be pleasing to the goddesses and spirits.

Add water to a pot and then simmer the following herbs and oils on the stove, stirring as they heat:

- Dried apple slice
- Rose petals
- Fresh pine needles (chopped)
- Cedar tips or oil
- Juniper oil

Exercise: Celtic Goddess Incense

This incense can be burned on a coal or used to dress a candle, consecrate a sacred vessel, or as a pleasing invitation to goddesses in other rituals.

Crush the following herbs and combine them with a few drops of your favorite oil to create an incense that can surround your altar and act as an invitation to goddesses:

- Dried apple
- Rose petals
- Pine resin
- Cedar tips
- Juniper berries
- Hawthorn flowers
- Mugwort
- Lavender
- Rosemary

Exercise: Celtic Goddess Bath Soak

Use this simple bath soak to relieve stress and tension, and to prepare yourself for rituals that invoke the goddesses:

- 1 cup Epsom salt
- 1 tsp baking soda
- 3 drops cedar essential oil
- Rose petals
- Crushed juniper berries
- Slices of fresh apple (with pentagram showing)

PART II

Goddesses of the Sacred Waters and Landscape

CHAPTER 5

Sulis—Goddess of the Gap

Name variations: Solimara, Sulevia, Sulevias, Sulevise, Sulevis,
    Idennica
Region: Bath, England
Sacred associations: Celtic—the number three, second sight, pigs,
    liminal spaces; Roman— hippocampus, owl, coins, libation
    bowls, jewelry
Offerings: aquamarine, carnelian, images or trinkets of the sun,
    coins, cabochons, bowls, meat, liquids like wine, jewelry
    and gemstones, plates, owls, military paraphernalia, carved
    wooden and leather objects, effigies, tablets, food and drink,
    clooties, circumambulation
Body of water: thermal springs in Bath, England

Sulis, whose name means "eye of the sun" or "goddess of the gap," is a goddess of liminality, of in-between spaces, of the realms unseen. She is the goddess of light and shadow, sun and darkness. She is the radiant solar goddess of the sacred thermal springs. Her symbols include the sun, springs and wells, hot springs, the gorgon, serpents, curse tablets, hippocampus, owls, and (a modern association) the vesica piscis, a mathematical shape formed by the intersection of two circles (see Figure 14).

There are various interpretations of what Sulis's name means. Some believe that it derives from the proto-Celtic word *sūli*, which means "sun." And certainly, her steaming waters, which bubble up packed with healing minerals that leave a deep orange sediment, corresponds well with this solar association. Others believe it may be derived from the Old Irish word *súil*, which means "eye," denoting an inclination toward perception and perhaps second sight. Because this goddess is also associated with the sacred number three, this connection with the eye and sight may suggest a third nature, intuition, or deep oracular work. In fact, the word can also be taken to mean "hope" or "expectation." And this may make sense, because water's reflective surface can reflect back an image and thus communicate a message. But the word can also mean "gap," indicating the unknown nature of what lies deep beneath the waters—perhaps a portal to the Otherworld.

It is unlikely that we'll ever have a definitive answer as to the true origin of Sulis's name, and many choose to honor all three aspects of the goddess in their work. What is clear, however, is that Sulis is neither an underworld deity nor an above-world deity. She rules over the gap, the liminal space. She is both here and there, in and out. She is the goddess of the sun and the subterranean waters—and all the places between.

Sulis is both a fire goddess and a water goddess, reigning over the solar realms as well as the realms of aquifers and the dark damp earth. It is believed that there was a perpetual sacred flame kept burning within her temple, much like Brighid's. She is deeply connected to the light and radiant warmth of the sun, but also to the underworld where her warm waters originate. Here, we will explore this great goddess in her many aspects—as a goddess of life and death, a goddess of cursing and healing, and a goddess of nurturing and fertility. We'll also consider other goddesses and mythologies that can give us clues to her worship.

Sulis appears in the records of the Bretons, the Gauls, the Romans, and the Anglo-Saxons, and continues to play a role in the practices of modern priestesses and Pagans. First and foremost, however, she is a Celtic goddess—a steady and steadfast singular goddess whose worship has brought many to her magical healing waters. Although she can also be classified as a Roman goddess, it is important to remember that her worship originated in the Celtic culture and that the thermal springs at ancient Bath, where water has been bubbling up at the rate of nearly 240,000 gallons a day at a temperature of 46°C since time immemorial, have remained one of the most famous healing shrines of the Celts.

During the Roman occupation of Britain, which began in roughly 43 CE, the Romans destroyed many Pagan sites. Yet they built a temple complex to Sulis at Bath around 60 CE, preserving her traditions by appending the name of Minerva—their goddess of wisdom, justice, and strategy who was also associated with music, medicine, crafts, and magic—creating the hybrid goddess Sulis Minerva. This was contrary to their normal practice of changing the names of local gods and spirits, indicating that Sulis was a local deity of immense importance—what the Romans called a *genius loci*. With the help of Roman engineering, this site was expanded into a vast temple complex, ensuring that worship of the goddess continued across time.

After years of Roman occupation, the temple fell into ruin and disrepair, and was almost forgotten until its rediscovery in the Victorian era, when it came into use again by aristocrats as a vacation destination and spa. Now, the sacred site at Bath is one of only a few surviving Roman temples in Britain, and people across many cultures go there to worship the goddess and partake of her healing waters. At the site, you can visit the Roman ruins, which have been turned into a museum that contains one of the only remaining artifacts of Sulis—a gilded bronze head discovered in 1727 (see Figure 3). You can also visit a modern-day spa that uses her sacred waters in a theraputic way. The spa includes pools, saunas, and steam rooms, one of which has a beautiful mosaic of Sulis on the back wall.

Unfortunately, only a few small inscriptions and altar stones dedicated to Sulis remain and there is little historical evidence of the practices of her ancient Celtic followers, although a few remain within the Roman temple ruins where some partook of the Roman practices. Although hundreds of curse tablets were found at her shrine in Bath, as well as hundreds of votive offerings given to honor her, only two inscriptions to Sulis have survived, one by a sculptor indicating that his work was a gift to the goddess. Nevertheless, today, her temple is visited by hundreds of thousands of people and she is worshiped by Pagans and polytheists worldwide. Indeed, Sulis has re-emerged from the depths of her waters to shine once again as Britain's Celtic solar goddess and guardian of the sacred thermal springs.

Evidence of large-scale animal sacrifices has been found at the temple site in Bath, along with over 12,000 coins. Certainly, a spring that poured forth hot orange-tinged water was not only strange, but spoke of something deep and magical in this place. We know for certain that the Celts believed that Sulis's sacred waters were life-giving and tied to the very sacred nature of the landscape.

Figure 3. Bronze bust of Sulis discovered in the 18th
century at the temple site in Bath, England.

It is interesting that there was also a school of medicine located in Bath during its early days. It seems a reasonable assumption that a mineral spring that was visited by many to heal various ailments would also attract physicians who may have used the water in their own work, although there are no records to support this. A "medicine stamp" discovered in the abbey churchyard around the mid-1700s was briefly passed into the hands of antiquaries who made three cast impressions of the seal. Sadly these three reproductions and only one old text now document its existence; the original has been lost. Today, a variety of modern and traditional healing and relaxation techniques are offered to visitors at a spa that is located close to the Roman temple complex, including massage, steam rooms, hydrotherapy, and warm pools that continue the sacred work of the water goddess.

Celtic Goddess Grimoire

Sulis is truly a multi-faceted deity who deserves to be honored and revered at her site and in our own homes. She is England's goddess, and her legacy lives on in modern Paganism and in other traditions today. A few priestesses are dedicated to honoring the sacred well cult that is so revered in the United Kingdom and other parts of Europe, working with her, keeping her waters on their altar, and honoring her and her sacred springs.

GODDESS OF HEALING AND CURSING

As we have seen, Sulis was a goddess of many aspects. Although she is known primarily as a goddess of healing, she can also bring the swift sting of a curse. Healing isn't all love and light, after all. Sometimes healing occurs when a stolen item is returned or a wrong is righted through the force of a powerful goddess. There is a deep healing that can take place within the depths of darkness. Sulis's dynamic nature shows us her ability to heal in a loving gentle way when necessary. But there are times when the poison must be sucked out, when the shadow must be subdued, or when the cause of trauma must be pulled out by its roots. This kind of healing requires complete transformation, and Sulis stands prepared to hold you fiercely as you tumble through the deep waters of life until you are cleansed and polished, like a beautiful cabochon stone that was found in the drain of her temple complex.

Although Sulis is most often connected with solar energies, she is no stranger to the dark. And it is important to remember that her sacred waters originate in the dark nocturnal world of aquifers deep below the ground. Here, in the silent darkness of the deep earth, her iron-laden waters flow forth from three separate routes reaching down into the aquifer, a dark womb-like cavern deep in the ground. Because of this, those who menstruate may wish to connect with or honor her during this time. For those who have experienced a miscarriage, the loss of a child, or sexual trauma, she can be a comforting aid during times of pain and through the tumultuous darkness of deep healing. She embodies the vast spectrum of energies, from the deepest darkest recesses of the earth to the shining solar energies above. She can nourish you or burn you with her hot rays; she can adminster the waters of life or drown you in their depths. Like the source of her sacred springs, she is deep and powerful, and she demands that her priestesses and children be so as well.

Although we don't have any specific references to Sulis being a goddess of battle, the Roman conflation of her with Minerva certainly connects her to these attributes as well. In fact, among the artifacts found in the temple ruins at Bath were over 150 *defixionis*, or curse tablets, most dating from the third and 4th centuries CE, that contain petitions seeking justice or revenge. These thin lead tablets were inscribed by petitioners and then folded several times to conceal the writing before being tossed into the sacred waters. Sometimes the words were concealed by covering them, sometimes by writing backward with a mirror, sometimes by simply scribbling unintelligibly. This protected the secrecy of the curse.

Reciprocity was also an important part of these rituals—the giving of gifts, the taking of vows, and the promise of petitioners that, if the request was granted, they would undertake an act of gratitude like making a votive offering or perhaps sacrificing an animal. Thus these tablets represented a kind of contract between the deity and the petitioner. Generally, this contract was dictated by a scribe but written by the petitioner, perhaps indicating that, for the curse to be effective, it had to be written in the petitioner's own hand. This practice has survived in modern witchcraft as a "taglock," an item or object that belongs to the petitioner—a precious item, spittle, hair, name and birthdate, hand writing, nail clippings, etc.

I have personally experienced Sulis to be a powerful goddess of wisdom, protection, and strategy. Those who work to protect the waters of the earth may find her to be a valuable ally in their work and can seek her aid in matters pertaining to protection magic and legislation related to preserving our planet's water.

RELATED GODDESSES

As we have seen, Sulis, although most often considered a solar goddess, has a darker side as well. Thus, her temple contains a depiction of the lunar goddess Luna. And this is not the only place we see Sulis linked to lunar energies. For instance, on the Isles of Scilly, located off the coast of Cornwall, are the ruins of a Romano-Celtic civilization called Nor'nour. During the excavation of this site, a statue was found that is an effigy of the goddess Sillina, who is considered to be a sea goddess linked to Sulis.

Another goddess who may be the same as or similar to Sulis is Xulsigiae, an obscure Gallo-Roman water goddess who has been lost to time. This little-known goddess has connections with solar energies and mother archetypes, and has been known to appear in triplicate. She is also connected with sacred healing springs. Xulsigiae is connected to male solar and fire deities, and shares some similarities with other goddesses of sacred healing springs like Sūliās and Suleviae, whom scholars suggest may be versions of Xulsigiae through her connection to solar energies, sacred springs, and her tripartite aspects. However other scholars are adamant that Suleviae has no connection with Sulis and should not be conflated with her.

There is a shrine to Xulsigiae in the temple of Lenus Mars in what is now Trier, Germany. This shrine was built near a sacred mineral spring that flows through the temple complex. The temple was home not only to Xulsigiae and Lenus Mars, but to his consort, Ancamna, and to the *genii cucullati*—Roman-Celtic spirits often found in groups of three, many times wearing cloaks and hoods. Depictions of these spirits appear repeatedly in Celtic, Roman, and Gallic water temples, especially those associated with solar deities or with inscriptions and dedications to solar spring goddesses.

While it does seem that much of the temple at Trier was focused on Lenus Mars and his consort, an inscription to Xulsigiae found there indicates that she was not only a powerful goddess of healing, but was also considered a figure worthy of vow-fulfillment. The inscription translates as:

To Lenus Mars and the Xulsigiae,
Lucius Diseto freely and deservedly fulfilled his vow.

It is interesting to note that, in this inscription, the name Xulsigiae is preceded by "the," perhaps indicating a grouping or a goddess in triune form. This may link Xulsigiae to the *genii cucullati* or the three mothers or three nymphs. Remember that Xulsigiae is linked to Sūliās and her triune form as Suleviae. She may also have been considered to be a mother goddess and may have been connected with wisdom, maternal rule, or legal matters.

It's not uncommon for powerful solar deities who are also connected to thermal, mineral-rich, and sacred springs to have a connection with a set of three or nine water nymphs. Thus, it is possible that the name "Xulsigiae" refers to a group of three nymphs as well as to a solar goddess. Indeed, some scholars suggest that Xulsigiae is another version of the triune goddess

Suleviae, who is sometimes characterized as a home and hearth deity, linking her with domestic sacred-flame goddesses like Vesta, Hertha, and Brighid. This may also link her to other triune mother goddesses and goddesses of fertility. And it is possible that she is connected to mother goddesses through her similarities to the Matronae and the Matres, who often appear in triune form (see chapter 12).

What we do know is that Xulsigiae was honored by Romans, Celts, Gauls, and Germanic tribes in many different guises and forms. And we know that sacred springs, solar deities, and water nymphs played a prominent role in Greek and Roman religion, and were also central to practices of the Britons and Gallo-Romans. Thus Xulsigiae, no matter whether she was worshiped in triplicate, as a nymph, or as a powerful solar goddess of healing and sacred waters like Sulis, is a dynamic goddess connected to other Celtic deities and their associations with sacred springs, solar energies, and the sacred number three. She can thus be honored in our modern practices by placing solar objects, sacred water, spring water, and the sacred number three upon her altar. Depending on how you want to work with her, you can also reach out to her energies as a water goddess, a mother goddess, a fertility goddess, a triune water nymph, or as a sacred solar goddess who brings abundance and prosperity to the land.

A variety of sacred practices that honor Sulis are still performed today. Many of the well practices found in the archaeological record can be adapted to honor her in a modern context, including votive offerings of coins, tablets, food, and drink, as well as clooties (see chapter 6) and circumambulation of sacred wells and springs. Even some well practices that are not particularly associated with Sulis can be used to honor her, as they were practiced by those who lived and worshiped in these places and by their descendants. Here are just a few examples of rituals that you can adapt to your own practice.

Exercise: Honoring Sulis

One of the best ways to begin honoring Sulis is to create a shrine or altar space dedicated to her and her sacred waters. There's no wrong way to do this and each person will find different ways to decorate this sacred space. In my temple space, I use the colors displayed in the waters and stone of her temple—a sandy tan color and a rich blue-green similar to the waters in her main bath. I know people who use cobalt blue to represent her aspect as a water goddess and some who use a strong red to connect with her solar and fire aspects. Or you can use a combination of yellow and black to connect with the solar and nocturnal realms. Just choose the color that feels right to you and that supports your individual style.

Your altar surface is also up to you. Just remember that the surface you choose and what you put on it make a difference. If you want to honor the goddess's fire aspect by placing candles or an oil lamp on her altar, be careful not to place them under a shelf or near any flammable materials. If you are honoring her water aspect by placing a bowl or dish of water on the altar, don't use a surface that can be marred by water. You can also choose to dedicate a space in your yard near a fountain, a bird bath, or a creek.

Once you have selected your surface, consider whether you want to use an altar cloth or keep your surface natural. If you are burning candles, be sure to safeguard your altar cloth from dripping wax, as it can ruin most fabrics.

Your altar to Sulis can contain a number of different items associated with her worship, including a statue or image of the goddess, a watery feminine figure, a bowl or sacred vessel to hold water, candles or an oil lamp, effigies and images of owls, pitchers to pour water, bottles to store sacred water, offering bowls, representations of the sun, items that may connect you to her temple, coins and jewelry, flowers and offerings of fruit, and gemstones like citrine, carnelian, aquamarine, quartz, and pearls (see below).

Try to connect with Sulis each morning to invoke her sun aspect and give her weekly offerings. If you place water on her altar, make sure it is properly blessed. If you leave offerings of food, drink, flowers, or fruit, be sure to refresh them regularly.

Exercise: Sulis Spell Bottle

You can create a spell bottle to use in rituals that call on Sulis's various healing powers by combining sacred water from Sulis's temple or another sacred spring source with a gemstone that is associated with your intent. Here are some examples:

- Choose aquamarine for healing and to connect with Sulis's water aspect.
- Choose citrine to raise your energy and honor Sulis's solar aspect.

- Choose quartz points for inspiration and to enhance healing.
- Choose pearls to transform bane to beauty and to heal old wounds.
- Choose shells to call on ancestral waters, for protection, and to invoke the spiral of healing.

Cap the bottle tightly and move it in a clockwise (sunwise) circle over your altar three times, while speaking this invocation to the goddess's healing powers:

> Goddess of light, and goddess of healing water,
> I invoke you now, in your many forms,
> Of heat and cool, of light and dark, of flame and water.
> I invoke you now, Sulis.
> I invoke your healing powers and the presence of your grace.
> Lend me your power in this healing hour.
> Wash me with your healing waters.
> Take away the pain and nourish me with the warmth of your flame.
> Help me here in this hour of need;
> Bring about healing with great speed.
> My heart is filled with gratitude,
> And I am honored to have your wondrous presence here in this
>   sacred space.
> Thank you for lending me your grace.
> So mote it be.

You can adapt these words to your own practice and intent, or create your own prayer of dedication or blessing.

Place the bottle on your Sulis altar and use it for saining (see chapter 6), to anoint yourself or objects before or during rituals, or to add power to a sacred bath.

Exercise: Sunrise with Sulis

Here is brief ritual that honors Sulis's sun and fire aspects by meeting the rising sun each day with a brief invocation to the goddess.

Each morning, take a vessel of spring water and place it in the light of the rising sun. Let it sit for a few minutes with the light flowing directly on both you and the vessel. Then take nine sips of the water, and sit and meditate on the light and power of the sun. Call on Sulis, goddess of both thermal springs and the sun, using the invocation below or words of your own choosing. Meditate on the power of solar water and the light that refracts and glitters on its surface. When you are finished, take nine more sips of water, then gift the rest to the earth.

Feel free to adapt this brief invocation to suit your own practice and intent.

You who are the goddess of the in-between,
Arise from the depths of the aqueous realms unseen.

Exercise: Spell to Seek Sulis's Blessing

Sulis can be petitioned for a wide variety of blessings. You can do this at your own altar, at a body of water like a lake or a river, or at a sacred well or spring. The process is much the same, no matter where you reach out to the goddess. This exercise can be adapted to all kinds of prayers. Just change the herbs to suit your own practice and your intent.

First, cleanse your altar space or the site where you will be working by saining with holy water made from a hag stone. This can be any type of stone that has a natural hole made through it by the erosive force of the moving water of a river or the sea. Look for one in a dry riverbed or along the seashore. These stones have a long history of use in protection magic and make great protection amulets because they retain the beneficial power of the water. Simply place the hagstone in a bowl of spring water overnight.

Place a candle on your altar or in a safe place at the site where you are performing the spell. Crush herbs appropriate to your intent. I often use a combination of eyebright, calendula, and chamomile, but you should adjust the herbs to your own practice and the blessing you seek. Anoint the candle with rosemary oil and then sprinkle the herb mixture on the candle. If you wish, you can speak an incantation as you do this—something appropriate to your intent. I whisper my incantations as I place three fresh mini roses and fresh orange rose petals in a circle around the candle for the final touch.

Be sure to spend time in communion with the goddess and give any offerings that you feel appropriate.

Exercise: Solar Tea Ritual

Here's a simple ritual you can do to honor Sulis's solar aspect.

For this, you will need:

- Chamomile
- Calendula
- Rose
- Peppermint

- Eyebright
- 3 tumbled citrine stones
- 3 tumbled sun stones
- 3 tumbled carnelian stones

Place the dried herbs into a large jar with a lid. Pour spring water into the jar and cap the jar tightly.

In the morning around nine o'clock, take the jar outside and place it in direct sunlight. Arrange the nine stones so that they alternate—citrine, then sun stone, then carnelian—all the way around the jar. Leave the jar in the direct sunlight for three, six, or nine hours.

When you retrieve the jar, strain out the herbs and offer three small splashes of the tea to Sulis. You can do this on your altar or directly into the earth. Then enjoy your tea!

Exercise: Sulis Ritual Bath

Ritual baths are a great way to prepare yourself before a ritual, as well as to cleanse yourself after one. They can also be used just to make yourself feel good. Here's a formula that you can use—either in your practice, or just for relaxation.

Combine the following ingredients with some Epsom salts:

- Chamomile
- White sandalwood
- Dried calendula
- Dried yarrow
- Peppermint

- Jasmine
- Cedar oil
- Fresh rose petals
- Fresh rosemary

Fill a tub with comfortably warm water and add your herbal mixture. Then just climb in and enjoy the experience.

When you step out of the tub, let yourself dry in the air for a few minutes before you pat yourself dry with a soft, clean towel.

Exercise: Quick Healing Ritual

For this ritual, you will you need:

- A candle

- A bowl

Celtic Goddess Grimoire

- A citrine crystal
- Water from a sacred spring or spring water made into moon water (see chapter 7)

- 3 quartz points

First cleanse your altar by asperging or saining with holy water and sacred herbs as described on page 47.

Next place the bowl on your altar in front of the lit candle. Place the citrine in the bowl and pour the spring water over it. Place the three quartz points around the bowl with the points outward to create three rays or a triskele-like shape. Hold your hands over the bowl, charge it with your intent, then ritually anoint your body with the water from the bowl. Call on Sulis for healing as you do.

CHAPTER 6

Brighid—Goddess of the Sacred Well

Name variations: Bridget, Bridie, Brigindo, Brigantia, Brixia, Brieta, Saint Brigit, Bríde, Bríd
Region: Ireland, Scotland, England, Wales, Isle of Man, continental Europe
Sacred associations: wisdom, poetry, healing, protection, smithing, the forge, oak, sacred wells, sacred flames, midwifery, rivers, domesticated animals, hazelnuts
Offerings: keeping a perpetual flame, spring water, devotional poetry, Brighid's crosses, bridie bed, oat cakes, bannocks (Scottish flatbread), milk, cream, butter
Bodies of water: Ireland: St Brigid's Well, Kildare; Brighid's Well, Mullingar, River Boyne, Leinster. England: White Spring, Glastonbury; River Brent, London. Scotland: Iona's Well, Iona. Wales: River Braint, Anglesey. The River Danube and many, many more.

Brighid is probably the most popular Celtic goddess with the widest worship in ancient and modern times. Today, her worship is found worldwide and reaches far beyond Celtic practices. She is revered and honored in Ireland and Scotland, and in Cornwall and other parts of England as well. Although her story originates in Ireland, it is hard to box her into one particular region, as she is honored in many places across the Celtic landscape. Information on Brighid abounds on the Internet, in books, and in modern-day worship practices. In fact, there are several books that are dedicated just to her. Because of her popularity, I have intentionally kept her chapter short. If she calls to you, I highly recommend finding a book dedicated to her and studying it.

Brighid is a mysterious goddess, and there is comparatively little information about her, which is ironic as she is currently among the most beloved of the Celtic goddesses. Cormac's Glossary indicates that she is one of the Tuatha Dé Danann. This is what is known from the ancient myths: Brighid is the daughter of Dagda. No references to the identity of her mother exist. Brighid's husband is Brés. They have a son named Ruadán. Following the death of Ruadán, Brighid is credited with inventing keening, the ancient Celtic rite of mourning and grief. Brighid may be one of three sisters who share the same name, an indication that she is possibly a triune goddess. These three sisters are associated with healing, smithing, and poetry. There is also a Saint Brigid; goddess and saint are often conflated with each other.

Throughout the ancient and modern Celtic world, Brighid is recognized as a goddess connected with sacred wells. Scholars suggest that the ancient Celts believed that the landscape they inhabited—the island of Britain itself—was a goddess. Britannia may thus have been a British goddess of sovereignty who was perhaps also connected to Brighid. Early Roman coins depict a goddess named Britannia standing on a globe with a sword and spear, and this name was used to refer to England during the 18th and 19th centuries. The same was true in Ireland, where the goddess Ériu is seen as the personification of the Emerald Isle.

Brighid is associated with wisdom, poetry, healing, protection, smithing, and domesticated animals. One chronicler of the 9th century describes her as "the goddess whom poets adored." Others report that she had two sisters, one of whom was a healer, one of whom was a smith. This suggests that she may have been a triune deity. With the advent of Christianity, she became identified with Saint Brigit, who shares many of the goddess's attributes, as well as her feast day of February 1, which was originally the Pagan festival of Imbolc.

Brighid has many sacred associations. She is considered a patroness of healers, poets, blacksmiths, livestock, and dairy workers, and is often linked with cows. She is associated with serpents in Scotland and in many locations she is linked to the arrival of spring because her feast fell on Imbolc, which marked the start of that season in Irish traditions. She is sometimes called Bridie in her maiden form and has an interesting connection with The Cailleach (see chapter 11)—an old woman of winter who dies and is reborn in her maiden form of Bridie at Imbolc. She is linked with springs and with fire, and is sometimes known as Brighid of the Eternal Flame, an epithet that dates back to the 12th century when Christian clerics kept a perpetual flame burning in Kildare to honor Saint Brigit.

Brigantia, a continental Celtic goddess, is widely believed to be a form of Brighid, although many scholars dispute this. In some ways, Brigantia is similar to Brighid, but seems to be her own figure and is not always connected to Brighid. In Gaul, for instance, she is worshiped as Brigindo, while elsewhere on the continent she is known as Brigantia. Another continental goddess worshiped by the Celts was Brixia, sometimes spelled Brieta, who may also be a form of Brighid. Only one inscription to Brieta has survived—at a thermal spring in southern France at a place called Luxeuil. The Romans conflated Brighid with Minerva, but sometimes called her Victoria and identified her with their goddess of victory. They also sometimes connected her with Caelestis, a sky goddess from Syria whose name means "the high one," and with other Celtic healing goddesses like Sirona and Coventina.

Today, Brighid has a large following devoted to her worship and she is associated with many holy wells and sacred springs worldwide. The most popular are located in Ireland—Brighid's Well in County Meath and Saint Brigit's Well in Kildare. In fact, many springs that may not have had ancient associations with her have been devoted to her in modern times, including White Spring in Glastonbury, a well that was dedicated as a shrine to Saint Brigit in the early 2000s, but was reconsecrated to Brighid several years later. Each Imbolc, a ritual takes place there in which a young maiden who is the embodiment of the goddess creates a sacred flame with straw and flint that is then carried into the dark cavern-like shrine and kept lit until the following Imbolc. This flame is used to light the candles that illuminate the shrine, which has no electric lighting. As a volunteer at this temple, I have the honor of keeping a backup flame in my home in devotion to the goddess and the sacred waters, just in case the flame goes out during the night when it is left unattended.

Below are some ritual practices you can use to invoke this versatile goddess.

Exercise: Invocation to Brighid
Use this invocation to call upon the goddess in her aspect as keeper of the sacred flame and to access solar energies:

Figure 4. Brighid's symbols on the White Spring gate.

Celtic Goddess Grimoire

Bridie of the sacred spring,
Your healing powers I ask you to bring.
Brighid, mother, midwife,
I seek your presence in my life.
Great goddess, I call upon your name,
Sacred keeper of the flame.

Exercise: Clootie Ritual for Healing

Clooties are small strips of cloth or ribbons that are left as part of a healing ritual, usually by dipping them in the waters of a sacred well or spring and tying them to the branches of a tree nearby while reciting prayers of supplication to the spirit who resides there. These locations are often places of pilgrimage and they are found across the Celtic world. Because clooties are associated with the waters of sacred wells and springs, they are an effective way to petition Brighid for healing and to honor her.

Traditionally, petitioners created clooties by tearing a piece of fabric from their clothing, preferably near to or associated with the area they wanted to heal. This is not practical in our modern world, however, for two reasons. First, you really don't want to tear your clothing and, second, because most clothing today is made with synthetic fabrics. The idea behind a clootie is that the fabric must decompose, and to tie fabric that does not decompose to a tree may eventually harm it or the environment. So when you do this ritual, be sure to choose a natural and not a synthetic fabric. You may also wish to wear the clootie on your body in some way to connect it with your energy.

To perform a clootie ritual, find a sacred or healing well near you. You can also use a spring if there are no healing wells in your area. As Brighid also has an association with rivers, you can use a river if that is all you have available. Take the strip of cloth to the location you have selected and ask the spirit of the sacred site for healing. Pray to Brighid and ask her for healing as well. Dip the fabric into the water three times; then find a tree that is directly next to the spring or that speaks to you. It may already have clooties on it. Tie the strip of wet fabric onto the tree and knot it three times, saying:

Water from the healing well,
Bless me as I do this spell.
I tie this clootie on the tree;
I knot it one, two, and three.

That which causes me harm
Leaves me now with this charm.

Leave appropriate offerings or clean any trash and litter from the area as an act of devotion.

Exercise: Saining in Brighid's Name

Saining is a Scottish word that means "blessing," "protecting," or "consecrating." Traditional saining rites usually involve the use of water and smoke, accompanied by ritual gestures and spoken or sung poetry and prayers. Thus Brighid's associations with both sacred waters and the eternal flame make her the perfect goddess to ask for blessings and protection during a saining ritual.

In a saining ritual, spring water that has been blessed in some fashion is sprinkled around using a bundle of fresh herbs that has been dipped into the water. Traditionally, Juniper is used, but I like to use whatever fresh herbs are in season. Rosemary and mugwort are great substitutions when Juniper is not available. Saining with smoke is usually done with large branches of burning juniper, either outdoors on a bonfire, or in a large vessel like a cauldron. Ceremonial gestures used in these rituals vary across Celtic traditions, while the prayers and invocations used are traditionally Gaelic. Saining was also used in healing rites. Today, it is a common practice used in rites based on Scottish folklore, like blessing and protecting children and other family members.

As you perform this rite, you can use your own words to ask for Brighid's blessing and protection, or you can use a prayer based on old saining charms, like this one:

Good Brighid, I seek your blessings.
Good Brighid, shield me and my home.
Good Brighid, protect me from every wound.
Good Brighid, tend to me as shepherds do their flock.
Good Brighid, take me under your glorious mantle.
Good Brighid, keep me and save me.

Exercise: Bridie's Bed

A traditional folk practice that I love to do in honor of Brighid is to create a little Bridie's bed on Imbolc using a straw or corn dollie to represent the goddess. In some of the traditional setups I have seen, the dollie is dressed in white and green—sometimes in a white dress with green ribbons. The dollie I personally use is a roughly ten-inch porcelain doll that I redressed. I place her in a little basket that is lined with pretty fabric. Some people add a little lace trim and blankets. I then add small offerings of biscuits, mini herbal bundles, and four-armed Brighid's crosses (see below).

Get creative and try designing and building your own Bridie's bed to honor the goddess and the coming of spring.

Exercise: Creating a Brighid's Cross

A Brighid's cross is a talisman that was common in Celtic devotional practices and rituals. These crosses, which generally have either three or four arms, were also worn as protective talismans and were sometimes given as offerings to Brighid.

To create a four-armed Brighid's cross to use in your own practice, you will need:

- Several traditional fresh-harvested rushes
- Clips or clothespins to hold the stalks in place
- Yarn to secure the stalks
- Scissors to cut the yarn and trim the ends

If you do not have access to fresh rushes, you can use dried wheat or rye stalks. If you use wheat or rye, soak the stalks in boiling water for several minutes until they are soft and pliable. Any material you use should be able to bend in half without breaking.

Take two stalks, bend each in half, and fold them together (see Figure 5A). Once they are interlocked, turn them so that they are at right angles to each other (see Figure 5B). Bend a third stalk in half and fold it around one of the first two, placing it at a right angle (see Figure 5C), then bend a fourth stalk in half and fold it around the third stalk at a right angle, so that, together, the four stalks create a four-armed cross (see Figure 5D).

Repeat this process, placing each new stalk parallel to one of the arms of the four-armed cross you created (see Figure 5E). Continue this process, folding each new stalk over the last one you added to each arm. As you add more and more stalks, you may want to use the clothespins or clips to hold them in place.

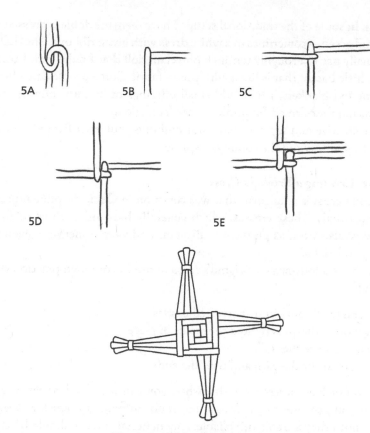

Figure 5. Making a Brighid's Cross.

When the cross is the size you want, tie the ends of the stalks together, securing them in place with the yarn. Adjust the stalks as you go to make sure they are tight and interlocked. Then use the scissors to trim the ends and make them even.

Exercise: Brighid's Mantle
Brighid's mantles are pieces of clothing that were used to bless and protect. They were often worn in rituals to honor the goddess.

To create a Brighid's mantle, place a consecrated scarf or a sacred robe outside on Imbolc Eve to catch the dew and receive Brighid's blessing. Then wear it for protection or to connect with the goddess during rituals.

CHAPTER 7

Arnemetia and Nemetona: Goddesses of the Sacred Grove

ARNEMETIA

Name variations: Arnemetiae, Arnamentia, Arnomecta, Arnemeze
Region: Buxton, England
Sacred associations: sacred groves, hot and cold springs, sacred springs
Offerings: coins, clooties, food, flowers, nuts and berries, libation
   bowls, effigies, rings, tree seedlings, bracelets, elaborate well
   dressings
Body of water: Aquae Arnemetiae—the springs in Buxton

Arnemetia is a little-known Celtic-Roman water goddess whose name holds within it the word *nemeton,* a Celtic word meaning "in the sacred grove." Her name can thus be translated as "water goddess of the sacred grove," or "waters of the goddess of the sacred grove."

Tradition tells us that, when the Romans arrived in Buxton, they found a Celtic shrine to a local spring goddess named Arnemetia. The Romans must have considered this place to be of great value, because they renamed it Aquae Arnemetia, a name they also applied to the temple to Sulis at Bath, which they called Aquae Sulis. For the Romans to give the site this name suggests that it may have been as important to them and to the local Celts as Aquae Sulis, the only other site renamed with the prefix *Aquae.* Moreover, Aquae Arnemetia and Aquae Sulis share several other similarities. As in Bath, the Buxton site contained more than one well—at least two or three, and perhaps as many as four—and at least one of these was a hot spring, as at Aquae Sulis.

Aquae Arnemetia became a popular thermal and healing spa. Like the more popular temple to the solar goddess Sulis, there was a heavy emphasis at this site on healing, and the spring was reported to have healing properties. It was especially known for healing gout. Although there is no great Roman temple complex in Buxton like the one dedicated to Sulis in Bath, the reputation of the waters for healing survived the Roman occupation and the site was heavily used throughout different time periods. Votive offerings like coins, bracelets, and other objects have been found there, as they were at another site in Bristol that also boasted a hot spring.

After the Roman era, and with the rise of Christianity, one of Arnemetia's wells was renamed in honor of Saint Anne, who may have been a Christianized version of Danu, an Irish mother goddess (see chapter 13). The site, which became known as Saint Anne's Well, was used as a source for drinking water as well as a place of secret meetings. It was said to be a place where those who opposed Henry VIII met in secret to plot against him. In 1536, Henry destroyed the site along with many others in an attempt to discourage this subversive activity, but it was re-opened by Elizabeth I after she began her reign in 1558. Elizabeth was responsible for transforming the sanctuary into a facility for therapeutic treatment and leisure enjoyment, adding a bath house and a thirty-room inn where mineral water was consumed and visitors played games and socialized.

When Mary Queen of Scots visited the well in the time of Elizabeth, she described the waters as milky white. But the well found in Buxton today is rich in minerals and iron, like the magical waters of Bath. Thomas Hobbes described the waters as hot and having sulfurous veins that brought to mind a watery flow of red blood, often giving these springs the name "blood spring." While there is no direct mention in the historical record of two distinct springs at Saint Anne's Well, one having red waters and one having white, this makes for an interesting connection to the sacred springs in Glastonbury. Today, there are several springs in Buxton besides Saint Anne's Well, including Crescent Well, Market Well, and Children's Well, which is also known as Taylor's Well.

The archaeological finds at the temple ruins in Buxton indicate that fitting offerings for Arnemetia included rings, bracelets, and coins, as well as offering bowls and effigies. Many other ancient and modern well traditions are also associated with this goddess. Today, Arnemetia is associated with the crowning of festival queens and well dressings.

Exercise: Forest Ritual to Honor Arnemetia

Trees and groves have long been associated with sacred springs and holy wells, and many were thought to have magical and spiritual properties. Here's an exercise that can help you connect with Arnemetia by partaking in a ritual of sacred waters in the sacred grove. In it, you will create two different types of magical water and take them to your favorite forest, grove, or tree, where you will bathe in the magical waters with the goddess.

For this ritual, you will need a towel, a ritual wash cloth, a bowl or sacred vessel, and a blanket, as well as some sun water and some Full Moon water.

To create Full Moon water, place pure water or water from a sacred source in a silver, white, or clear glass bowl and set the bowl out where it can capture reflections of light from a Full Moon. Let the light of the moon shine directly onto the water to imbue it with Full Moon energies. You can also add plants with associations to the moon or crystals like moonstone or quartz. Let the water absorb the energy from the moon's reflected light overnight, then bottle it and keep it cold in the fridge.

To create sun water, place pure spring water or sacred water in a glass or crystal bowl and set it out in direct sunlight for nine consecutive hours. This is best done on a Sunday, if possible. You can add plants, crystals, or symbols with solar associations to enhance its sun energies. When the water is fully charged, bottle it and keep it warm, or reheat it if necessary when you are ready to use it.

Prepare a basket or bag to carry the items you will use in the ritual to the sacred grove. Bring offerings of coins that you can take back and place on the goddess's altar; bring offerings of fruit, flowers, apples, and other local or seasonal organic fruits that you can leave for the animals where you perform rituals. I recommend dressing in something loose and light that can get wet, but that will still give you a degree of modesty that makes you comfortable. Place your warm sun water and your cold moon water in the basket as well.

When you arrive at the ritual site, first clean the area, removing any trash or debris. Then find a beautiful tree that calls to you or a space in the center of a few trees. When you have found the right spot, clear a space to

Figure 6. Nemetona's altar stone in Bath.

create a natural altar, then spread the blanket next to it. You can even select twigs, sticks, roots, and rocks to create a border, perhaps using grass, leaves, and flower petals to create the base of the altar.

Once you are satisfied, place your sacred vessel or bowl in the center of the altar and put the offerings you have brought with you around the bowl, adorning the natural altar space. If you have brought incense or candles, you can add them now, but be sure to remove all unnatural objects from the grove when you are finished so you don't pollute the environment. And be sure you are careful where you place them. Set both jars of hot and cold water near you.

When you are ready, begin by invoking Arnemetia:

Beautiful and radiant goddess, I call upon thee.
Arnemetia of the sacred grove,
Ancient healing goddess of the trees,
I call you from the depths below,
Deep within your watery flow.
Arnemetia of the healing spring,
I call you forth with love to bring.
Arnemetia of the sacred grove and holy spring,
Please be with me now.

Pour a third of the moon water into the bowl or sacred vessel, then sip from the bowl, ingesting the energies of the moon. Dip your ritual cloth into the bowl and wash your face, heart, hands, and feet with the sacred energies of the moon. Pour the remaining water on the ground.

Pour a third of your sun water into the bowl and sip from the bowl, ingesting the energies of the sun. Dip your ritual cloth into the bowl and wash your face, heart, hands, and feet with the sacred energies of the sun. Pour the remaining water on the ground.

Pour a third of the moon water and a third of the sun water into your bowl and mix them together while singing, praying, or offering words of devotion over the water. Then pour the mixture onto the altar you created, offering up the sacred waters of Arnemetia to the earth and the sacred grove. Speak out loud about your gift, your devotion, and your love for the natural world as you do.

Settle in and quiet your mind. Commune with Arnemetia by listening to her voice in the trees, by feeling the waters in your body. Tune in to the natural world and your inner knowing. What lessons does the goddess have to teach you? Does she whisper of the magic of the forest? Or of the mysteries of water? What lessons does she have to show you about the process of healing?

When you are finished with the meditation, pour the last third of both liquids into the bowl, mixing the energies of the sun and the moon. Bring the bowl to your lips and take three small sips, connecting with Arnemetia once more. Then lift the bowl above your head, tip your head back just slightly, and pour the rest of the waters onto your crown and forehead, allowing them to flow over your third eye, your face, your neck, and your chest and body as you speak this incantation:

> Waters of bone and waters of blood,
> Wash over me with a magical flood.
> Cleanse me like the trees do the sky
> And lift me from this dense earth to fly.
> Waters of blood and waters of bone,
> I call you forth from your forest's watery home.
> Heal me with your magical flow.
> Your blessings upon me, goddess, please bestow.

Clean up the site and leave the natural offerings to the local wildlife. And be sure to journey back to this sacred space to commune with Arnemetia again.

NEMETONA

Name variations: Nemeton
Region: Trier Germany, Klein-Winternheim near the middle Rhine River
Sacred associations: sacred groves, trees
Offerings: food, flowers, nuts and berries, rituals in her honor outside or in open-air temples, planting tree seedlings
Body of water: Rhine River (although she is not considered to be a river goddess, the veneration of Nemetona was located near the Rhine River)

Nemetona is another goddess of the sacred grove whose name translates as "she of the sacred grove" or "goddess of the shrine." She was worshiped in Germany by the Nemetes and is believed to have been their ancestral goddess. In fact, her name is sometimes rendered as "Nemeton." There is also an altar found to her in Bath—one that was placed there by a Gallic man who worshiped her at that location. While she is not generally considered to be a river goddess, evidence of her worship has been found in Trier, Germany, and in Klein-Winternheim, a municipality located along the River Rhine where the Nemetes lived. Thus she is often associated with this body of water.

Ritual practices to honor Nemetona are very similar to those for Arnemetia, but there are some differences. She is not associated with sacred springs, or at least no evidence survives other than her association with Arnemetia. She is connected more specifically with sacred groves and trees, and perhaps with the Matres Nemetiales, a group of mother goddesses who appear in triplicate who are known from a single inscription found near Grenoble in France. Appropriate offerings to Nemetona include food, flowers, nuts, and berries. Rituals to honor her include the planting of tree seedlings and she was most often worshiped outside or in open-air temples.

Exercise: Making a Wild Necklace to Honor Nemetona
Making a wild necklace is a great way to honor the goddess Nemetona. This is a lovely exercise that I have been using for several years.

String the seeds of trees onto a thread and allow them to dry. Tree seeds make excellent beads, and can be strung to create talismans and charms used for protection, luck, and beauty. I first thought of this idea when I wanted to connect with the spirit of a plant or a tree on a more intimate level. There is nothing more powerful than experiencing the intimacy of plant magic from seed, to sprout, to root, to fruit and berry, to winter dormancy. This magic can also be experienced by stringing nuts and berries onto a thread.

There are numerous ways to work this type of magic. First, it is important to note that not all nuts, seeds, or berries work well for this kind of practice. Berries like blackberries, raspberries, strawberries, and other soft fruits with small seeds are very hard to work with and you may have to use a dehydrator to make them viable. Even so, they may not work. Nuts and plants that have berries with more leathery skin, like rowan or hawthorn, tend to work well, but you have to be careful to make sure that, once they are strung, they do not molder during the drying process. You can even consider using peach pits. In general, try to use hard-skinned berries, fruits, or nuts. In some cases—for instance, when using hazelnuts, acorns, or fruit pits—you may have to drill holes before you can string them together.

If you decide to be creative with this exercise, go slowly and let spirit guide you. Some of my favorite berries to use are rose hips, hawthorn, and rowan berries because they are the easiest to string and dry. I have also experimented with crab apples with good success. I let the apples hang on a vertical string for several months in a dry place and rotate them every few days to let air circulate around them. Keeping space between the apples can help in the drying process.

Acorns and hazelnuts also work well, but you have to drill a hole through the center and the hard shell to string them. The advantage to these is that they don't require drying like berries. Ornamental cherries often have large pits and very little fruit, so they may also work well, although I haven't experimented with these. Nuts like chestnuts and walnuts work well, but I have not tried them, as they always seemed too big to wear.

Find out what types of trees grow in the sacred grove nearest you and use their fruits, nuts, or seeds to create a charm that can connect you with Nemetona. Once the necklace is strung and dried, wear it as a devotional piece to connect with the goddess of the grove.

Exercise: Journey to Nemetona's Sacred Grove

This exercise will take you on a vision journey to commune with Nemetona in her sacred grove.

Begin by closing your eyes, taking a deep breath, and relaxing. Count your breaths, starting at nine and counting backward to one. Bring your attention to your mind's eye and allow the day's distractions and any troubling thoughts to fade away. If you find any pressing thoughts coming into your mind, acknowledge them and then release them. Bring your attention back to your breath, feeling the sensation of your lungs expanding as you inhale and the air rushing out as you exhale.

You find yourself in complete darkness and look up and down, left and right. You only exist right here, in this moment. Soon, you see a tiny pinprick of light above you. As you gaze at it, it becomes brighter and larger, and you realize that you're looking at a beautiful golden orb that is spinning toward you. It rises up into the sky and turns into a fiery red-orange ball. It becomes so bright that you blink your eyes and rub them.

As you become accustomed to the brightness all around you, you feel a warmth touching your skin. You hear the sounds of birds chirping and insects buzzing. You see a butterfly hover right in front of you. It circles around and lands gently on your hand. You watch its wings flap slowly up and down, and marvel at their delicacy and intricate colors. You feel a light breeze begin to kiss your skin. You look down at your feet and see tall grass coming up to your knees. Then you find yourself in a field of grain. Little wildflowers give splashes of color here and there to the golden grain, which waves gently with the breeze, as if it were dancing to the sounds of the cosmos.

As you look around this beautiful field, you see a pathway in front of you—a narrow game trail that leads through the grain for as far as you can see. Without hesitation, you take one step forward and then another and another. Your feet move through the field, following the organic path back and forth, left and right, weaving in and out for what seems like a very long time. The sun is still bright overhead, but in front of you, you can see a dark shadow as a line of trees comes into view on the horizon.

Making your way toward these, you move out of the grain and into a field of wildflowers thick with bright colors and buzzing bees. As you follow the trail toward the looming trees, the flowers begin to thin and are replaced with rocks and bushes. In no time at all, you reach the edge of the forest. You look up at the tall trees looming overhead and begin to move through them, still following the trail that nature has laid out. You weave through maple and birch trees, looking at their beautiful leaves and elegant shapes. As you continue moving down the path, you notice that the sun is still shining, but is beginning to be obscured by leaves as the tree canopy thickens and becomes more dense as you move deeper into the tall trees.

Now you are moving between large trunks of pine, thick cedars, and clusters of twisted junipers. Giant trees rise up into the sky, creating a shade of darkness. The light peeks through here and there, bringing small rainbows to the dark mysterious wood. You move through the shadows, still letting one step follow another.

You find yourself in a beautiful grove. In the center, you see a circular shape—an opening of some sort. You move toward it and find a stone altar surrounded by nine beautiful trees that are leafed out in the foliage of all four seasons at once—each tree different, each one displaying its flower and fruit, each one being both vibrant with life and dormant at the same time. In front of each of these trees is a small dolmen with lines scratched upon it.

You move toward the first tree, an oak, and examine its leaves and nuts. Next you see a birch, then a maple, then a hazel tree, the tree of wisdom. Next to it is an apple tree hung with beautiful ripe fruit and delicate flowers. Beside it is a rowan covered in clusters of orange berries and white flowers; then a hawthorn, its long sharp thorns mingled with dense red berries and pungent white flowers. As you come full circle, you find an ash, and finally an elder tree full of juicy black berries and scented white flowers.

Which tree draws you in? Which one speaks to you? You listen to the trees and find that one reaches out to you. You go to this tree and kneel down before it, placing your hands on its roots. You allow your energy to become one with the tree, listening to the wisdom of the years, to the wisdom of nature. You take time now to quiet your mind and listen to the wisdom of this tree.

When you realize that your time with this tree is coming to a close, you say your final words and receive your final wisdom. As you thank the tree, you give it an offering—one strand of your hair—tying it gently to one of the branches. Then you thank the tree for its wisdom and for its time.

You turn back to the central altar and see the dancing flames of lighted candles that weren't there before. Beside them is a bowl of water, a needle, and a red thread. You move toward the altar, intrigued by what you see and, as you approach, your heart skips a beat. Your breath hesitates just ever so slightly and an intense energy flows over you. Before you, standing behind the altar, the most beautiful goddess you have ever seen appears—Nemetona.

She has long beautiful flowing hair mingled with vines, berries, nuts, and leaves. Her skin is soft, but has the texture of tree leaves. Branches poke out of her hair and vines wrap around her arms. The strange markings that you saw on the standing stones in front of the trees are displayed on her body, as if they were magical tattoos. Juicy berries and ripe fruit intermingled with flowers and fall leaves cascade down her body to form her clothing. Her feet are roots that are deeply connected to the earth.

The goddess asks that you water her and you agree. You move toward the altar and pick up the bowl of water. You speak a blessing, pouring your love and intent into the water, then you kneel down at her feet and gently pour the water over the roots that are one with the earth. You watch as the water is soaked up into her sacred body, then stand and place the empty bowl on the altar. She asks if you will water her children and protect those yet to come. But when you look down at the bowl, you see that it is empty.

For a few moments, you are unsure what to do; then you pick up the bowl and gently move it toward your body. You open your chest, your heart, your soul-center—the place where you store your love—and begin to pour that love into the bowl. You see water flowing from you into the sacred vessel. You walk over to the first tree and pour the water over its roots, just as you did for the sacred goddess, then move on to next tree. As each tree soaks in an abundance of water, you realize that the wellspring inside of you never runs dry.

Once you have watered all nine trees, you move back to the central altar and place the empty bowl on it. Before you close down the wellspring of your love, you let it flow one more time, leaving your essence there in the sacred grove and the temple of trees with the sacred goddess. She thanks you for your gift and asks if you will continue to water her children. When you agree, she reaches out her hand to you and, in it, there is a cluster of nine ripe nuts and berries from her sacred grove—one for each of the sacred trees. "This is my gift to you," she says. "Let it be a talisman that can connect you to me in the astral realm." You take the berries and, one by one, string them onto the red thread with the needle. The goddess takes the wild necklace and places it around your neck. You commune with her one last time, seeking any wisdom, advice, or instruction for service.

When you realize that your time in the sacred grove is coming to an end, you thank the goddess for her wisdom, knowledge, and guidance. As the candles begin to flicker and extinguish themselves, the beautiful goddess begins to fade as well. You move toward the opening where you first entered and begin to follow the little game trail back through the tall thick cedar trees, back through the maple and the birch, weaving in and out between the rocks and the bushes, until you once again reach the beautiful field of wildflowers.

As you move forward, the trees begin to disappear over the horizon and you find yourself surrounded by the beautiful fields of grain, still waving lightly in the breeze. The butterfly flutters by once again, this time moving up, up, up into the sky. You watch as it darts left and right and circles around, until you lose it in the brightness of the sun. For a moment, your eyes are blinded by the brightness of the sun and you close them and rub them and try to blink. Then the sun begins to fade and moves lower in the sky, casting shadows upon the land as if it were setting. You find yourself moving deeper into shadow, until all you can see is a tiny pinprick of light surrounded by nothing but darkness.

You bring your attention back to your breath, feeling the air flow in and out of your lungs. You feel your rib cage expanding and contracting. You bring your attention to your fingertips and your toes, giving them just a slight squeeze. You roll your wrists and ankles, and move your shoulders forward and back, then shrug them up to your ears. Then you gently flutter your eyes open and awaken.

While the memory of this sacred journey is still fresh, record your impressions in your journal. Which tree attracted you first? Which tree was nearest the altar? Which nuts and berries were you given by the goddess? What fruits and berries can you access locally to make into a sacred necklace?

CHAPTER 8

Coventina—Goddess of the Sacred Spring

Name variations: Dea Coventinae
Region: Hadrian's Wall in Northumberland; Narbonne in north-west Spain
Sacred associations: water, wells, fertility, dolphins
Offerings: coins, bone, glass beads, jet, bronze objects, leather, pottery, shale, lead, deer horn, figurines to bring rain for a good harvest and healing
Body of water: Coventina's Well in Brocolitia

Coventina is an interesting goddess about whom very little is known. Her shrine is found in the heart of the English landscape at the ruins of an old Roman fort along the famous Hadrian's Wall, which was built around 122 CE to keep the Picts at bay. This wall spans the entire width of northern England, from Maryport to Newcastle upon Tyne. Here, near the Roman ruins of Brocolitia, near the village of Carrawburgh in Northumberland, lie the ruins of a temple known as Coventina's Well. Although today the shrine is little more than rubble, many rich artifacts and devotional offerings have been found that were deposited there to honor the goddess, including 13,000 coins. Coventina's worship has been preserved primarily in altars and inscriptions left by Roman soldiers serving on Hadrian's Wall. One altar included a dedication to her, as well as the image of two dolphins.

The main site of Coventina's worship is near a spring that supplied a cistern. The site eventually became a temple that measured roughly thirty-eight by forty feet. The entrance to the temple lies in the west and opens directly into the center of the space, where there is a well that measures a little more than eight square feet. Near this well, there was a *mithraeum*, a temple where

Romans worshiped the bull-headed god Mithras, and a *nymphaeum*, a temple consecrated to water nymphs. Many offerings were found deposited in this well, including coins, leather, bronze and lead objects, bone, pottery, glass, shale, deer horn, jet jewelry, and figurines intended to bring rain for a good harvest or healing. Many of these offerings are believed to have been made by women petitioning for fertility and for a healthy pregnancy.

Other artifacts that have been found associated with the goddess include ceramic thuribles, vessels with a human head, and a relief of three nymphs. Shoes and shoe tacks were also recovered, which may have been thrown into the well so that the spirits of the dead would be properly shod in the afterlife. This indicates that Coventina may have had an association

Figure 7. Coventina's Well. A bas-relief found in
Carrawburgh dedicated to Coventina.

Celtic Goddess Grimoire

with death or was prayed to or petitioned to watch over the beloved dead. This, in turn, suggests an association with ancestral spirits.

Coventina's spring and its associated well, although they may have been known as a healing site, had no known healing properties. The water was not sulfurous and did not contain iron like the healing chalybeate wells. But it is hard to ignore the fact that sacred springs all over the Celtic world were most often associated with healing. In the case of Coventina, however, it appears that any healing that took place occurred through the intercession of the goddess and not through any healing properties in the waters themselves.

Exercise: Petition for Healing
Although little is known about the rituals and practices used to honor Coventina, it is safe to assume from the number of coins found at her well that people often petitioned her by offering her a coin. This exercise is a simple way for you to reach out to the healing powers of the goddess.

Charge a coin with your intent by placing it between your hands and speaking this prayer:

> Coventina of the well,
> Hold me in your spiral swell.
> A simple coin I give to thee.
> In return, I ask you hear my plea.
> Coventina, divine goddess, please heal me.

Place the coin in or near a well or other sacred site. As always, you can adapt this prayer to your own practice and intent. Or you can write one of your own.

Exercise: Petition to Protect the Spirits of the Dead
Because Coventina was thought to watch over the spirits of the dead, giving her an association with ancestors, you can petition her to watch over your loved ones who have passed by making an appropriate offering while speaking this prayer:

> Coventina, watch over the spirits who have passed,
> From the moment when they took their breath last
> To each and every moment ahead.
> Please watch over my beloved dead.

Coventina, please carry their souls
Through the Otherworldly waters' ebbs and flows.
Watery mother, please hold my heart
As I grieve those who had no choice but to depart.
Healing goddess, hold my soul's grief;
Allow it once more to feel as light as a leaf.
Coventina, in your watery flow,
Heal my grief and the tears of woe,
And melt the pain in me, as spring does snow.
To live with peace and keep grief subdued,
Coventina, please lend me your fortitude.

Exercise: Creating an Ancestor Altar

The sacred vessels displaying a head and the shoes found within the temple of Coventina indicate that, besides an emphasis on healing, Coventina may have been associated with death and, therefore, with the Ancestors. To honor your ancestors with Coventina, you can start by creating an ancestor altar.

In chapter 4, I gave general directions for creating an altar or sacred space. You can adapt these instructions to build an ancestor altar at which you can petition Coventina by focusing on the preferences and sacred associations of the goddess given above. Choose whether you want to keep your altar from prying eyes, or whether you will encourage sharing. Meditate and use your intuition to discover what the goddess's preference may be.

Choose a flat space or surface and decide whether or not you want to use an altar cloth. Then adorn the altar with appropriate items from the lists above. Since Coventina does not appear to have had fire associations, you can probably use a bookshelf, but if you want to place candles on the altar, be careful to use a space or surface away from any flammable materials. Since Coventina appears to have strong associations with springs and wells, be sure to include a vessel that contains consecrated water. Refer to the exercises in chapter 4 for instructions on how to bless a sacred image, anoint a candle, and consecrate a sacred vessel. When you are ready, dedicate your altar by speaking a prayer or incantation to the goddess. You can adapt the one given above or write your own.

CHAPTER 9

Elen of the Ways— The Antlered Goddess

Name variations: Elen Luyddog (Elen of the Hosts), Saint Helena, Elnias, Saint Elen of Wales, Elaine the Lily Maid
Region: England, Wales
Sacred associations: elecampane, birch, conifers, amanita muscaria, reindeer, deer, sacred springs and wells, trees, crossroads, ley lines, roads, bridges
Offerings: green objects, gold, copper, brass, deer antlers, lanterns
Bodies of water: Saint Helen's Well, Gwynedd, Wales; Saint Helen's Well, Yorkshire, England; Saint Helen's Well, Norfolk, England

Elen of the Ways is, to say the least, an enigma. She is an ancient spirit who has been lost to time. At the same time, she is alive and present in the lives of many today and still lives in the hearts and minds of those devoted to her. It may be a bit controversial to include her in a book on Celtic goddesses, as many will argue that she is neither Celtic nor a goddess. But this enigmatic spirit still appears in the practices of modern Celtic devotees, and her image can be found in almost every shop in Glastonbury, where magic and mystery run deep.

The goddess who is known as Elen has many names and stories associated with her. She is a beautiful antlered deity who travels the ley lines, alignments between significant sites that are now believed to demarcate earth energies. She is the spirit of the landscape—the one who shows the way, who illuminates crossroads. She is the spirit of the sacred springs. She is the Lady of the Greenwood, the maiden of the forest and the trees. She is a liminal spirit who stands between this world and the Otherworld. She brings forth life and mystery. She is ancient and, although little is known about her, whispers of her resonate across time. Her name is found in legend and lore, and echoes of her are woven into the tales of princesses, saints, and Otherworldly women.

The name "Elen of the Ways" was given to this ancient figure by author and devotee Caroline Wise to describe the mysterious and enigmatic goddess. However, she has been known by many names, including Elen of the Hosts, Helen, Elur, Elnias, Elona (she may be connected with Nehalennia), Saint Elen of Wales, Elaine the Lily Maid, and Saint Helen, the mother of Constantine. Today, many celebrate her on May 22, Saint Helen's feast day.

The information we have about Elen is scattered over time, across landscapes, and throughout history. Like many other goddesses and magical women, Elen is mentioned in *The Mabinogi*, where she is described as Elen Luyddog, or Elen of the Hosts, who was the wife of Emperor Maxen who built Sarn Elen, a 160-mile stretch of road that led from one castle to another. Although this road is attributed today to the Romans, tradition holds that it was ordered built by Saint Elen.

Elaine of Astolat, renowned as the Lady of Shalott, is thought to be connected to Elen as well. In fact, the Welsh word for "fawn" is *elain*. This heroine of Arthurian legend was immortalized in a Tennyson poem that has been influential in my own life and on my own personal path. I read this incredibly watery, magical, liminal, and transformative poem over and over to comfort myself in difficult times. It has also been sung in an abridged version by Loreena McKennitt. This song and poem have captivated audiences for hundreds of years.

What we do know about Elen is that she lives within the spirit of the land and in the hearts of those open to the mysteries of nature. Like many other goddesses and magical women in this book, she appears in many stories from different times, cultures, and lands. Although these tales are different, they all bear striking similarities. Elen can be experienced in many ways across many spiritual pathways, including ley-line work, and road- and bridge-building (real and metaphorical). She is connected with the forest, deer, and sacred wells. Many sacred springs across the United Kingdom are dedicated to her, including wells in Norfolk, Yorkshire, Lancashire, Staffordshire, Derbyshire, Essex, Lundy, Lincolnshire, and Wales.

Celtic Goddess Grimoire

But Elen's influence extends far beyond the British Isles. In Bulgarian, the word for "deer" is *elen*. She is also associated with the only female deer that has antlers—the reindeer—so she is connected with that animal as well. She is often associated with the amanita mushroom, which grows where birch trees and conifers mingle, making birch, pine, and other conifers sacred to her. Forest-marsh marigolds are often found growing in the waters of her sacred springs and elecampane may have been named for Elen or Helen.

Nehalennia, a marine goddess believed to be of Germanic or Celtic origin, may also be a form of Elen of the Ways. Evidence of worship of this goddess and numerous shrines and inscriptions to her have been found in the Netherlands.

Exercise: Invocation to Elen

Although little evidence survives of devotional practices used to honor Elen, it is clear from folklore and tradition that she can be worshiped in rituals that show a reverence for the sacred landscape and the natural world. Her aspect as the shower of ways and her associations with crossroads, lanterns, and ley lines also indicate that she can be petitioned for guidance and way-showing.

Here is an invocation to this enigmatic spirit that you can use to reach out to her for guidance on your path:

> Enigmatic Elen, I call upon thee.
> Green maiden, antlered one,
> Golden brilliance like the sun,
> Show me the tracks that are straight
> When life is too hard to navigate.
> Forest goddess, please show me the way;
> Show me the path upon which to stay.

As always, adapt this prayer to your own practice and needs. Or write one yourself.

Exercise: Road-Building Meditation

Begin by finding a comfortable position. When you're ready, close your eyes and begin to breathe rhythmically. Allow yourself to focus on the sensations of the air moving in and out of your lungs. Let go of any worries, stress, or frustrations from the day. Focus on releasing each thought as it comes into your mind. Then bring your attention back to your breath, focusing only on your inhalations and exhalations. Listen to the sound of your breath as it enters and leaves your body.

When your mind is quiet, look around in the darkness of your mind's eye. You look up and down, left and right, searching all around you for a sign of light. Turning slowly, you search, hoping to find a light behind you—any spark that can show you the way. As you turn, you see a tiny pinprick of light in the darkness. You move toward it—slowly, step by step, placing one foot in front of the other. As you do, this tiny pinprick of light becomes bigger and brighter. It begins to shift left and right as it approaches. Soon you find yourself staring at a single flame that is dancing inside an old lantern. The lantern is made of copper, its glass panels frosted and scratched with age. There are green patterns on the copper where it has begun to tarnish. Nonetheless, it is quite beautiful when the light from the single flame inside flickers and dances, creating magical reflections on the metal.

As you move your eyes away from the flame, you see that the lantern is hanging on the branch of a tree. You take it and hold it out in front of you to illuminate everything around you. You find yourself at the base of a large oak tree whose thick and twisted branches loom overhead. You look up to the sky and can barely make out the shape of a thin crescent moon. The stars seem to twinkle, but are mostly obscured by a canopy of trees. You observe dense intertwined branches and their thick clusters of leaves.

Holding the lantern high, you search for a pathway, desperate to find any sign that can show you the way. You take a deep breath and ground down into your center. Using your intuition, you begin moving through the thick trees, away from the ancient oak. Finally, holding the lantern high, you find a path. You give a deep sigh of relief, feeling confident and excited to see such a clear path before you. The path is wide. All of the sticks and rocks have been cleared from it. There are no roots or ruts to make you stumble. It is a broad and inviting pathway that is illuminated by the tiny dancing light in your lantern. You move down it confidently, knowing that something awaits you at its end.

As you walk, you contemplate life in the physical world. You think about the choices ahead of you that must be made, and how they will impact your soul and your life in the spirit realms. You remember that you've been faced with hard choices before. In the past, when you had to make difficult decisions, you often felt as if you were being pulled from one side to the other—torn in two with indecision. But the path before you is so clear that you continue to walk it. Thinking about how clear the path is gives you hope. Even though you are stuck right now, you can still find guidance and choose the right direction.

As you pore over the possibilities and outcomes of the choices ahead, your mind becomes confused and muddled by so many options, just as it did before. As you begin to feel bogged down by the heaviness of the decisions you must make, you notice that the path, like your mind, has become narrow and cluttered with rocks and sticks. You now have to watch where you put your feet as you walk, as each step could make you stumble. Each rock has become an obstacle. Each root growing out of the ground may trip you.

The pathway continues to narrow, so you hold your lantern higher trying to illuminate the way. The path now looks treacherous, winding left and right. And just as you begin to ask yourself where you go from here, the path forks—not just once, or twice, or three times, but an infinite number of times. And each fork presents different possibilities leading to countless different possible outcomes.

You find yourself at a great crossroads, a junction in the spiritual highway. Feeling lost and unsure which direction to go, you lower your lantern toward the ground, hoping to have just a few moments to breathe and decide which path to take. As you do, the lantern falls out of your hand and crashes to the ground, shattering into pieces. You are left in the dark, with no light to illuminate the paths in front of you. You don't feel comfortable choosing any direction without the light of the lantern. Without the light to guide you, how will you find your way?

Upset and frustrated, feeling alone and lost, you cry out into the darkness. "Please! Please! Someone help me to see the way. Please! Please! Someone show me the way. Please! Please! Illuminate the path I should take at this moment in time." Frustrated, you sit down next to the broken lantern and begin to sob. The choice is too hard to make with no light to see. So you close your eyes and wait in the darkness for help and guidance.

After a time, you hear the crunching of leaves. Then the gentle snap of a twig prompts you to open your eyes. Before you is a bright light that illuminates the forest around you and there, in the center of the light, is the magical feminine spirit known as Elen. She is beautiful, dressed in a green dress and a hooded cloak. Bits of dried berries hang around her wrists and a belt made of vines encircles her waist. Flowers twisted in her hair create a crown, from which her beautiful antlers ascend toward the heavens.

You look up and ask if she is there to show you the way. She reaches her hand down to you and you take it. She helps you up and then moves with you to the center of the fork in the path. She holds her lantern high and says: "I ask that you look again, and see the pathways when they are illuminated by my light." You begin to look at each path, following each possibility through time and space to its outcome. But the influx of information doesn't help much. If anything, it makes it even harder to choose. She patiently says: "Look again; look closer. Stop looking for the possibilities. Tell me which pathway belongs to you." She holds her lantern high again, illuminating all the possibilities in front of you.

As you look more closely, you see that one pathway is a little brighter than the others—a little greener. It feels inviting. It begins to pulse like a heartbeat. She smiles and says: "Yes, you see there are always unlimited possibilities. We are all made of unlimited possibility. But just because something is possible doesn't make it the right path. Just because a path is good doesn't mean that it's the path for you This time, before you look at the paths before you, close your eyes and listen. Listen to the rhythm of your heartbeat. Listen to the song of your soul. Listen to the words of nature."

You close your eyes and find you can hear a heartbeat like a deep drumming and thrumming within your mind. You can feel the pathway—the inviting, brighter pathway—pulsing as if to match your own heartbeat. The beautiful antlered maiden holds her bright lantern high above you and, when you open your eyes, you can see the heartbeat in the land. You can see your own heartbeat within that pathway, as if it sings a song straight to your soul. You take a moment to watch and listen to the wisdom of the path that has been illuminated.

After a time, the beautiful spirit gently takes your hand and says: "Shall we walk this path together for a while? Shall I illuminate the way to make it easy for you? For even though this is the pathway that matches your heartbeat and sings the song of your soul, it's easy to get lost. Sometimes the way is too hard, and you may want to turn around. So let me walk by your side and light your way."

She gently takes your hand and you begin to walk the path together. After you have gone some distance, she turns to you and says: "Our time is now coming to an end. It's time for me to leave you now. But take my lantern. Take my light, for, with it, you can illuminate what lies before you. You can avoid unnecessary fear. And if you ever feel lost, you can call me by name. Just raise the lantern high and say: 'Elen, show me the way; illuminate the path I should take. Build the bridge that will take me where I cannot walk.' I will come and light the way for you always."

You take her lantern and, like a thick mist, she fades softly into the trees. Her eyes and her antlers are the last to disappear. As you let your gaze move from the misty maiden to the dancing flame in her magical lantern, it looks as if the flame splits and you can see her figure within, the tips of flame forking up into two antlers. And you know that she will guide you when you're lost, when you are lonely, when you feel as if the light is gone and may never come back. You know that she will guide you.

You walk along the path until you are tired and you decide to rest on a bed of moss and forest flowers. You hang the lantern on a low branch. It illuminates the little violets and tiny pink flowers that are sprinkled across the green moss below and invites you to lie upon them. With the lantern burning brightly at your head, your eyes begin to grow heavy; the light fades and you find yourself in darkness. You find yourself in silence. You fall fast asleep. But you know that, when you are ready to resume your journey, you will have the guidance you need.

Bring your focus back to your breath and focus on the physical sensations of the air moving in and out of your lungs. Allow your chin to drop gently onto your chest and slowly move your head backward. Then begin to move it from side to side. Give your toes a little wiggle and your fingers a little squeeze. When you're ready, roll one shoulder backward and then the other, bringing movement into your body and allowing yourself to come back to this time and space.

CHAPTER 10

Melusine—Mermaid Goddess of the Fount

Name variations: Melusina
Region: England, France, and Scotland
Sacred associations: wild boar, sinew, magical rings, bath tubs,
    pearls, angelica, gemstones, shapeshifter, dragon, faery woman,
    mermaid, serpent, the number three, sacred springs and founts
Offerings: water from a sacred spring or fount, roses, flowers,
    pearls, angelica cakes
Bodies of water: the Fountain of Thirst and a spring in Lusignan,
    France

Melusine is a complicated goddess because, while we have her original story in a French text that dates back to around the 13th century CE, it is said that she was born to a Scottish king and raised in Avalon, which is believed to be in Glastonbury, England. To confuse things even more, we also have numerous other tales of her from around the world. She has been found in German fairy tales and may even be linked back to Greek mythology. And if this isn't complicated enough, there are many variations of her story spanning a number of different regions and times, some of which conflict with the French original, some of which complement it, and some of which are downright strange! Melusine even makes it into *Grimm's Fairy Tales*, where she appears in the little-known story of Herr Peter Dimringer von Staufenberg.

Melusine is reputedly the maternal ancestor of the hereditary line of Lusignan, whose descendants became Kings of Jerusalem during the Crusades. Another tale has her founding and building Luxembourg and claims that her descendants include Jacquetta of Luxembourg and her daughter Elizabeth Woodville, who became queen consort to Edward IV of England. Some versions credit her with the building of Notre Dame cathedral in Paris, while others place her at the Fountain of Thirst in the French woodland, although we will never know the exact location of this. In modern times, we see Melusine crowned in full glory in the Starbucks logo. There is even a street in Seattle, Washington, near the Starbucks headquarters named for her sister Palatine.

Melusine is a dynamic goddess who is deeply connected with the landscape, and especially with water. She is sometimes worshiped as a goddess of fertility and is associated with dragons, serpents, mermaids, sirens, and sacred springs. Her main lessons are sovereignty, magic, building, betrayal, faith in yourself, overcoming curses, and love.

In the French version of Melusine's story, a beautiful water nymph named Pressina married a Scottish king. Before she took her vows, she told him that she would only marry him on one condition—that he never look at or even attempt to look at her during childbirth. It didn't take long for Pressina to become pregnant. When she had delivered a daughter, the midwives realized she had another child in her womb. After they delivered a second daughter, they went to tell the king. In his excitement at being the father of twin girls, he rushed into the room just as Pressina delivered a third daughter. Angry and devastated, she gathered up her three daughters—whom she named Melusine, Palatine, and Melior—then jumped out the window and took them to Avalon, where they remained until they were fifteen years old.

As the daughters grew up in the sacred groves of Avalon, they became curious about their father and asked their mother about him. When they learned of his betrayal, they became angry that they had been robbed of the opportunity to be raised as princesses at court. So they decided to punish their father by turning him into stone. When Pressina learned what they had done, she became so angry that she cursed them. Melusine was cursed with growing a serpent's or mermaid's tail each Saturday; Melior was doomed to watch over her father's stone body for all eternity; Palatine was locked in a tower guarded by a flesh-eating hawk.

Melusine's story picks up again in the middle of a forest at a magical fountain in the middle of the night. It is here, at the Fountian of Thirst, that she first encounters Ramondine, who had inadvertently killed a dearly loved uncle while out on a wild boar hunt. Stricken with grief, he wandered through the forest, eventually coming upon Melusine and two other faery women at the fountain. After a series of magical events, Melusine agreed to marry Ramondine on one condition—that he never seek her out or ask where she is on a Saturday. Although this was admittedly a strange request, he immediately agreed to it and they were wed.

Melusine and Ramondine lived quite happily for some time. The land was fruitful and everyone who lived there was happy with how the realm was growing in strength and prosperity. The happy couple had ten strong sons, and all seemed well. That is, until Ramondine's brother arrived one Saturday to warn his brother of gossip he had heard claiming that Melusine was being unfaithful to him. At first, Ramondine refused to believe his brother, but then doubt crept into his mind and he decided to look for her and see what she was doing. He went to her chamber and peeked through the keyhole. To his dismay, he saw his wife in her mermaid form taking her weekly bath in her private pool. Shocked at what he saw, he sent his brother away with angry words and told him never to come to court again.

Although Ramondine never said a word to his wife about what he had seen, she knew that he had betrayed her. Nonetheless, she decided not to leave him because, although he had broken his promise, he did not betray her secret. Not long after, however, the couple's sons were struck by a series of misfortunes, and Ramondine became so distraught that he lashed out at Melusine in front of her handmaidens, betraying her secret and blaming her for the tragedies. On hearing this, she leaped through a window and sprouted great dragon wings and a long tail. Then she circled the castle three times and flew off to the mountains. She returned only to herald the coming death of someone in her family line by releasing the cry of the banshee.

Because of her strong associations with water, practices to honor and receive blessings from Melusine usually contain the element of water. On pages 87–89 I give you three, but you should be creative and find ways to honor her that fit well with your own practice and intent.

Figure 8. Sacred spring at Chalice Well in Glastonbury, reputed to be the legendary site of Avalon, where Pressina fled to raise her daughters Melusine, Melior, and Palatine.

Celtic Goddess Grimoire

Exercise: Sacred Bath to Seek Melusine's Blessing

Because of her strong associations with water, it shouldn't be surprising that a sacred bath is a great way to honor Melusine and call down her blessings. Ritual bathing can also be a great way to cleanse and refresh your body while you relax and restore your mind.

For this one, you will need:

- Organic rose petals
- Oil of rose, rosemary, or evening primrose
- A bathtub
- A silver coin or a small silver object
- A sacred vessel
- Spring water, preferably natural spring water

Be careful not to use petals from roses bought in a store. They are often dyed or full of chemicals and pesticides that help them retain their perfect shape. Thus they remain free from the small flaws that often come with exposure to nature. Consider using roses you picked yourself in a garden or dried organic rose petals.

Begin by placing a sacred vessel on your altar and filling it with spring water. Hold the silver coin between your fingers and stir it clockwise in the water three times while saying:

One, two, three times about,
All good come in, all evil go out.

Then drop the coin into the water and leave the bowl on your altar while you are preparing your bath.

When you are ready, cleanse your tub area. Add candles to set the mood if you like. Fill the tub with water, then hold the bowl that contains the silver coin over the water and invoke Melusine, using these words or others that fit your practice and intent:

Faery maiden, spirit of the spring,
In your name I now sing.
Shapeshifting goddess of fertility,
I ask that you bestow your magic upon me.
I call upon you now, Mother of Water,
To commune with your sacred daughter.

Mother of sacred spring,
Grant me the strength of your dragon's wing.

Pour the water from the bowl into the tub, sprinkle the rose petals into the bath water, and add your chosen oils. Then step in and relax.

Take your time and enjoy the bath. Perhaps sink into a contemplative state or take a vision journey to visit Melusine. Indulge yourself—perhaps with a glass of wine and some chocolate. Focus on your intent. When you are ready, step out of the tub and let yourself dry in the air for a few minutes before you pat yourself dry with a soft, clean towel.

Exercise: Beauty Bath

For this bath ritual, blend all the ingredients below in a small dish or bowl so they are ready to pour into the tub. You may want to grind the herbs into a fine powder using a mortar and pestle.

- Epsom salt
- Baking soda (1 tablespoon only)
- Rose oil
- Rose petals
- Lavender
- Calendula
- Angelica

Again, be careful not to use petals from roses bought in a store. When you are ready, use the invocation above while sprinkling your ingredients clockwise into the water. Then step in and enjoy the experience.

Exercise: Charm Rings

This ritual can be adapted for any magical charm, pendant, or talisman you want to enchant. For it, you will need a sacred vessel, some natural spring water (preferably collected from nature, but you can also use bottled water from a store), and a silver coin or small silver object. This can be any object you choose, but it must be silver. You will also need a ring or another object that you want to charm, as well as a few appropriate offerings for the goddess.

On a Full Moon, set an altar space for Melusine. In the center, place a sacred vessel of your choosing and fill it with spring water, When you are ready to begin, approach the altar and invoke Melusine using the invocation above or one you write yourself.

In your dominant hand, hold the silver coin or silver object and stir the water with it three times in a clockwise (sunwise) direction. Then place the coin or silver object in the water, saying:

I swirl this silver three times around
In this sacred spring water from the ground.
Melusine sweet and fair,
Lounging in water, combing your hair.
Sacred spiral I turn around thrice,
To bring forth your magic I do entice.
Silver coin like the shining moon,
Bless this water with the siren's tune.

Place the ring or object to be enchanted in the water. Hold your hands over the sacred vessel and ask in your own words for Melusine to imbue the ring or object with magical power. Be sure to be clear about whether you are asking for luck, for love, for prosperity, or for protection. You may wish to enter into a light trance and speak directly with Melusine.

Once you feel the ritual is complete, leave your offerings, the sacred vessel, the silver coin or object, and the ring or object you charmed on the altar overnight. The next morning, retrieve the ring from the water and place the silver object in your cleansing basket to be cleansed later. Pour the remaining water into the earth as an offering to the land.

CHAPTER 11

The Cailleach—Giantess

Name variations: Cailleach Bhéara (Irish), Cailleach
  Bheurra (Scottish Gaelic), Black Anis
Region: Scotland, Wales, Ireland, Isle of Man, Spain, Iberian
  Peninsula
Sacred associations: weather, storms, winter, mining, sovereignty,
  death, war, the wild woman, wild nature, deer, foxglove
Offerings: corn dollies, storm water, bowls of snow or melted
  snow water
Body of water: Well of The Cailleach

The Cailleach defies all categories. She is a giantess and a goddess of the landscape. But she is sometimes seen as an Ancestor associated with the creation of the landscape and with the weather, especially storms and winter. She is often depicted as the personification of winter and is linked with stories of giantesses from across the British Isles and throughout Europe. Her name literally means "old woman" or "hag." She appears in numerous mythological and folkloric tales in Ireland, Scotland, and the Isle of Man, although her origins come from a Greek text that indicates her connection to a Celtic tribe called the *Kallaikoi* that lived in the Iberian Peninsula. It is also possible that she is of Maltese origin, as speculated by Sorita de Este.

The Cailleach is variously known as a creator goddess, a storm goddess, and a destroyer, and as a giantess who can move large boulders, make mountains, raise the seas, and create windstorms. In Wales, she is connected with mining. Locations associated with The Cailleach include Loch Awe in Argyll and Bute on the Isle of Skye. The Lochaber mountains are named

Beinn na Caillich in her honor, while Cailleach Bhéara is associated with Hag's Head in West Cork and with Ceann Caillí on the Cliffs of Moher in County Clare. The Hag's Mountain in County Meath and Sliabh na Caillí are associated with her as well, as are the fords at the River Orrin. Many locations claim to have their own Cailleach—for instance, Cailliach Mhór Chlibhrich, Great Witch/Hag, and Giant Cailleach Point on the coast of Mull. Cailleach nan Cruachan is said to live on the peak of Ben Cruachan.

According to Ronald Hutton, the word "Cailleach" derives from the Old Irish *caille*, which originally meant "veiled one," relating to a faithful wife or nun. Later meanings include "older woman" or "old married woman," and these meanings eventually evolved into "hag." Thus The Cailleach came to be seen as a hideous female figure who haunts wild and lonely places and performs spells. Few traces of her survive in medieval literature, although more survive in later folkloric texts. In the 9th-century text *The Lament of the Old Woman of Beare*, she appears as a hag of sovereignty and speaks as the crone, lamenting her lost youth. She is often described as a mother or crone goddess and was seen as a protectress of the forest, nature, and animals. She was associated with death, war, the wild woman, and wild nature, and is seen in some traditions as representing the destructive forces of nature. Miaran nan cailleacha síth—thimble of the old faery woman—is another name for foxglove, the beautiful flower that grows throughout the British Isles and thus may be sacred to her.

The Cailleach's connection with deer appears in the figure of Cailleach Beinne Bhric horò, who is described as a broad tall figure who had a herd of deer that she didn't let feed on the black weed of the shore, feeding them instead on the watercress that grew near a spring in the hills. These deer are often called "faery cattle," making it difficult to tell if they were actually cows or deer.

The only shrine to The Cailleach that has survived is located in a place called Glen Lyon, which was originally named Gleann Lìomhann ("the valley of Lugh") for the warrior-king Lugh. Deep within this valley is place called Glen Cailleach where the oldest known shrine to her still exists. We don't know when this shrine was established, but it is believed to be an ancient site.

A curious ritual still takes place at this site each year in a small stone hut called Tigh nam Bodach. Inside the hut are a family of sandstone figures that have been shaped by the elements. One stone represents The Cailleach, one represents her husband (Bodach, "the old man"), a third is named for their daughter, Nighean. There are a number of other stones there as well that are believed to represent more of her children. Each Beltane (the Gaellic May Day festival), those who honor The Cailleach take the stone family out of the hut, arrange them outside, and leave them there until Samhain (November 1), when they are returned to the hut for the winter. Scholars believe that these figures may have been linked to farming and fertility rituals, because The Cailleach was known to watch over cattle and help increase the yield in the fields. She was also known for prosperity and fertility.

Exercise: Using Storm Water for Protection
In this exercise, you will collect storm water to create a protection water that you can use to wash your windows, doors, and floors. If you have any left, you can use it for offerings. For this, you will need three stones of equal size—ideally a red one, a white one, and a black one. These may be hard to find. I have had trouble finding them myself, only to stumble upon all three at once on a beach I hadn't even planned to visit.

To begin, place a vessel outside before a storm and let it fill with storm water. Put all three stones in the water and chant this invocation over the vessel:

Spell woman,
Giant woman,
Goddess of the herd,
Storm mother,
Stone mother,
Goddess of the wild,
Winter crone,
Snow crone,
Goddess of the night,
Cailleach, faithful crone of sovereignty,
Please protect my loved ones, home, and me.

When you are done, take a small amount of the water and pour it out as an offering. Use the rest to wash your floors, then dip your hand in the water and create spirals (counterclockwise to close and protect) on your windows and doors. You can also draw a protective bind rune, a pentagram, or a triskele instead. This water is excellent for use in protection magic.

Exercise: Harvest Spirit Doll

This exercise is inspired by an old custom called *Cailleach-bhuaineadh*, which means "the old woman of the harvest." In it, you will make a harvest spirit doll that you can give as a gift of prosperity to a loved one who is lacking in abundance. To create the doll you will need dried corn husks, string, some yarn, and scissors.

Begin by soaking the dried corn husks in hot water. Once they are pliable, take a small handful of husks (about three to five) and tie them together, leaving one to two inches of husk at the top (see Figure 9A). This will become the dollie's body. Fold the top of the husks down over the string to create a ball-like shape for the head. Use the string to secure this shape in place and set this piece aside (see Figure 9B).

To create the arms, make a thin bundle from two to three husks and tie off each end with the string (see Figure 9C). Sometimes I like to braid the arms and you can do that as well. Then insert the arm bundle into the dollie's body, just below the head (see Figure 9D). Finally, tie yarn around the center of the dollie to create a waist and a skirt and to secure the arms in place (see Figure 9E). If you want to create legs instead of a skirt, split the husks below the waist into two sections and tie the sections with string to create knees and ankles (see Figure 9F).

You can add clothing using yarn, fabric, or leaves, or decorate the dollie with jewelry and other adornments. You can even put a rock or crystal in the head and sew on hair made of yarn, but this is best done as you create the body. Or you can tuck a written prayer into the belly before you tie the yarn around the center to create the waist.

Once you are happy with how the dollie looks, place it on your altar and bring it to life. Place your hands over the dollie and visualize it coming alive. Take a deep breath and blow air over the dollie's head to "give it its first breath of life." Sprinkle it with your favorite holy or magical water and dedicate it as a spirit home for The Cailleach. Then give this dollie to loved ones with instructions to keep it in their home and feed it often with love, offerings, and prayers.

Celtic Goddess Grimoire

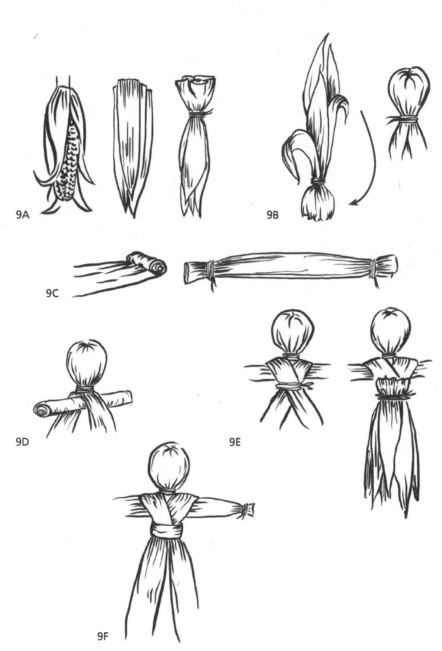

9A

9B

9C

9D

9E

9F

Figure 9. Making a corn dollie.

PART III

Goddesses of Abundance, Fertility, and Healing

CHAPTER 12

The Matres

Name variations: Dea Matronae, Matres Suleviae, Matres Come-
dovae, Matronae Aufaniae, Matronae Vacallinehae
Region: northwestern Europe, Germania, eastern Gaul, northern
Italy, Rhineland, Britain
Sacred associations: patera, midwives, snakes, birds, children, bowls
or baskets of fruit, decorations of plants and trees, incense,
prosperity, nurturing, bread
Offerings: incense, burnt sacrifices, fruit, cornucopia, distaff
Bodies of water: River Marne in France, thermal springs at Aix,
sacred springs

Many goddesses in the Celtic world can be identified as mother goddesses,
but perhaps the best known are the Matres, also known as the Matronae,
who were worshiped in Britain, northwestern Europe, and particularly
along the length of Hadrian's Wall. *Matres* is a Latin word meaning "mothers"; *Matronae* is a Latin word meaning "matrons."

Evidence of worship of these mother goddesses has been found that
dates from the first to the 5th century CE. They are depicted on nearly 1,100
votive offerings and altars that bear their images—generally in groups of
three, indicating that they were sometimes considered triune. In most cases,
these have been found in clusters around temple buildings and worship sites.
While about half of the inscriptions on these artifacts bear Celtic names,
many of them give Germanic names, indicating that these goddesses were
also venerated in regions of Germania, eastern Gaul, and northern Italy.

When depicted in groups of three, these goddesses are generally shown
either standing or sitting, with at least one figure holding a basket of fruit. In

some cases, the middle figure is shown with loose hair and wearing a head-band, while the other two wear headdresses. Some scholars suggest that the loose hair may indicate maidenhood, while the headdresses may indicate married women. The consistent presence of a basket of fruit seems to represent these figures as triune fertility goddesses, a motif that was widespread throughout Europe in figures like the Fates, the Muses, and the Charities. The same theme appears in Hinduism as the *Tridevi*.

Sometimes the Matres are referred to as *Dea Nutrix*, meaning "nourishing goddesses." In other cases, they are given the epithet *Domesticae*, which may indicate their role as deities of the homeland, but also may indicate their role as mother goddesses. When depicted in groups of three, they are sometimes shown as identical and sometimes appear with varying hair or at different ages. Other associations include snakes, children, bowls of fruit, decorations of plants and trees, and burnt sacrifices, including incense. The snakes may refer to an association with the souls of the dead or the under-world, while the children seem to suggest that these deities served to protect the family. They may also have been identified with midwives.

The Matres also seem to have a significant connection to the goddess Dea Matrona, who is connected to the River Marne in France and who is cognate with Madron and possibly Morgan le Fae (see chapter 21). Dea Matrona, however, appears as a single goddess rather than in triplicity, although her name also means "mother goddess" or "divine mother goddess."

The information that survives about the religious practices surrounding these goddesses is sparse. However, there is no doubt they are linked with fertility, motherhood, and abundance. While altars and effigies have been found, no mythology or folklore that relates specifically to the Matres, Dea Matrona, or the Matronae has survived. Our knowledge of them is limited primarily to the artifacts found at their worship sites. The exercises I give here come from my own practice, but are grounded in what we know about these mysterious mother goddesses.

In 2018, I had a profound healing experience at Cross Bath, which is near the ruins of the Roman temple complex in Bath. While sitting in Sulis's sacred waters, this great goddess claimed me as her own, showing me that she was my true mother. I was her child and always had been. I went straight to her temple—what is now known as the Roman Bath Museum—and walked around in a daze until it was time to leave. The next day, I woke up

Figure 10. The Matronae represented as three figures.

and walked out to the Chalice Well gardens where I was staying in Glastonbury and spent the day with the goddess, journaling and meditating. Before I left, I went to the Mother and Child statue there to do a ritual (see Figure 11 on page 104). On the next page is a variation of that ritual. I hope it brings you comfort and peace.

I have placed this ritual here with the Matres, but you could perform it to honor Sulis or any other mother goddess found in this book. I now repeat it on Mother's Day, but you may prefer to perform it on Mother's Night (Mōdraniht), which is Christmas Eve.

Exercise: Healing the Mother Wound

Mother's Day isn't an easy day for many. Many of us have lost our mothers or are estranged from them. If this is the case for you, try your own version of this healing spell.

In my own practice, I use the following ingredients:

- Healing incense blend (choose one from your favorite shop or create your own)
- Rosemary burning bundle
- A glass dish
- An oil of your choice
- 3 motherwort leaves (you can also sprinkle dried motherwort)
- An orange flower
- Chalice Well water (or any spring water, preferably collected directly from the sacred source)

Motherwort can be a powerful plant ally in healing wounds relating to mothers. The orange flower aligns with Sulis's solar aspect, but I encourage you to use a flower that feels right for you and aligns with the goddess you are honoring. It can also represent your mother or the goddess whose comfort you seek. Feel free to come up with your own mixture, one that best fits your intent.

Begin by lighting your healing incense blend. Light the rosemary herbal bundle and cleanse your altar space with smoke. I do this in the pattern of the pentagram. You can also dip the bundle into spring water and sain the space by sprinkling the water on your altar.

Place a flat dish on the center of your altar. Arrange the three fresh motherwort leaves on the dish in a three-pointed motif. If you don't have access to fresh motherwort, sprinkle dried motherwort in the shape of a triple spiral or a three-pointed pattern. As you do this, align your energy with the three divine mothers—the Matronae. Contemplate healing the mother wound by forming three strong links to the mother goddess. You can also interpret the three-pronged shape to represent yourself, your earthly mother, and the Divine Mother. Or you can view each branch of the shape as representing one of the three Matronae.

If any negative feelings arise as you do this—past pains or traumas—that's okay. Allow yourself to process these feelings. If they become too strong, use sacred smoke or saining to cleanse away the negative energies.

When you are ready to move forward, hold the orange flower in your hands and, in your own words, seek the Divine Mother's blessing. Contemplate the beauty of the flower and ask to form a relationship with the mother goddess you are petitioning. Take a deep breath and, as you exhale, blow it out onto the flower. Do this three times, then place the flower on the dish in the center of the motherwort. Pour the spring water over the dish in a clockwise direction, nourishing the ritual and the relationship you are forging. Finally, place three drops of your chosen oil into the center of the flower.

When you are finished, put the flower and the motherwort somewhere where it can dry, then crush them and keep them in a vial on your altar. Pour any remaining water into the earth.

Exercise: Charm Bag for Fertility
This spell is for those who may be having trouble conceiving a child. If you are seeking to adopt, you can keep this charm bag with your adoption paperwork or carry it with you during interviews and stressful times. There are many ways to create a charm bag and you can use any one you prefer in this spell. However, I have also provided one below.

In a green bag, place a magnet, motherwort, a gold or silver coin, a shed snakeskin, eggshells, and basil. To amp up this charm bag even more, add a vial that contains sexual fluid from both you and your partner. Bless this bag with spring water or silvered water (see chapter 10).

Once you have created the bag, place it in the center of your bed between the box spring and mattress, or as near as possible to the place where you intend to conceive. Then say this prayer before and after your fertility check in the morning, and before and after each attempt to conceive:

Matres, Matronae, mothers in triplicity,
Your blessings I implore.
I seek to become a mother deep in my core.
Matrona, Divine Mother, hear my plea.
May your fertility swell within me.

Figure 11. Mother and Child statue at Chalice Well in Glastonbury.

CHAPTER 13

Danu, Domnu, Dôn— Goddesses of Fertile Waters

Name variations: Ana, Anu, Dana, Dan, Ăna, Donand, Danann, Saint Anne, Black Anis

Region: Dane Hills in Ireland, River Danube

Sacred associations: mother goddess, abundance, cat, hare, rivers, primordial waters, liquid flow, dew, fertility, wisdom, wind, prosperity, breasts, knowledge, land, fertility, Cassiopeia, stars and constellations

Offerings: river water, dew

Bodies of water: River Danube; River Dnieper; Saint Anne's Well, Whitstone, Cornwall River

Danu is an Irish mother goddess who is often associated with water and has a deep connection to motherhood. She is sometimes conflated with Anu, although some scholars disagree, seeing them as completely separate goddesses who were merged early on. Some believe that "Anu" is simply a variant spelling of "Danu." Some believe that the name is derived from an old word for "knowledge," while others believe it means "to run" or "to flow." Regardless of how you view her name, it is clear that this goddess is a mother goddess who is deeply connected with Ireland. In fact, Danu is the mother of the supernatural mythological race of the *Tuatha Dé Danann,* which translates as "people of the goddess Danu." This mythological race was associated with living under the hills or the Otherworld. Their supernatural abilities and their agreement to move under the hills associated them with the faery realms.

Danu is quite interesting because, although she is an Irish mother goddess and there is no doubt that she is connected with the sacred landscape there, she may have been worshiped across many locations, cultures, and times—even as far away as India. Indeed, she may possibly have originated there. In Hindu mythology, a water spirit named Danu is connected with primordial waters and the waters of heaven, and was sometimes personified as trickling liquid or dew. In this context, her children were called *Dānavas*. The Egyptians wrote of a tribe called the Danuna that may also be connected to the Danaiis from Greek mythology. There may even be a connection as far back as the ancient Sumerians. The God King Anu, who is mentioned in the ancient epic of Gilgamesh, had a wife named Antu. Gods changing gender through the eyes and experiences of the cultures that worshiped them is not new.

Danu is deeply connected with the Celtic landscape and there are several locations in Celtic lands that are associated with her, including the Dane Hills in Leicester, which are said to be haunted by the hag Black Anis, and the Dá Chic Dannan, two identical hills in southwest Ireland also known as the Paps of Anu. These are thought to resemble breasts because they have prehistoric cairns on top of them that look like nipples. This association with breasts also appears in Llanmihangel, Wales, where there is a sacred well named for Saint Anne, who is believed to have been syncretized with the goddess Anu. Here, she was depicted in the wall of the fountain with her nipples gushing water. Sadly, this image is now obscured, but the documentation remains.

The name of the River Danube may have been derived from the name of this goddess as well. There is a possible connection in later folklore to Black Anis, the blue-faced fearsome hag who is said to live in a cave called Black Anis' Bower, where she lies in wait for unsuspecting children in order to ambush them and eat them.

As noted above, Saint Anne may be a syncretized version of Anu, having been merged into the role of Jesus's grandmother, and there are holy wells in numerous locations that are dedicated to her. Just as the Romans often conflated their goddesses with local Celtic deities, the Christians often conflated Celtic goddesses with the holy women of their traditions. This is one of the reasons why we have so many different Saint Anne's wells throughout the British Isles.

DOMNU

Domnu is an obscure ancestral Irish goddess who was said to have arisen from under the sea or the earth and was thought to represent the balance between the forces of good and evil. She is believed to be an Otherworldly goddess associated with the ocean and her name means "deep."

Domnu is mentioned in the *Book of Invasions* as the mother of the Fomorians, who were described as monsters who predated the Tuatha Dé Danann. These associations appear to connect her to Danu, hence her mention here.

DÔN

Dôn is a Welsh mother goddess associated with abundance, rivers, fertility, wisdom, and the fertility of the land. Like Danu, the mother of the Tuatha Dé Danann, she is the mother of the Welsh gods, who were sometimes called *Plant Dôn*, which means "children of Dôn." It is important to note, however, that, although they may be linked, Danu and Dôn are two separate goddesses who have many similarities.

Dôn is associated with the constellation Cassiopeia. In fact, *Llys Dôn*, which translates as "the court of Dôn," is also the Welsh name for that constellation. In Welsh texts, we see that castles, or caers, were often connected to or associated with particular astrological bodies. For instance, the castle of Gwydion, one of Dôn's five daughters, was associated with the Milky Way; the castle of Arianrhod, another of her daughters, is linked with the Corona Borealis or the Northern Crown. (Her other daughters were Gilfaethwy, Gofannon, and Amaethon.)

Like Danu, Dôn has strong associations with a river that bears her name, the River Dôn. She is honored with offerings of river water and with images of stars—specifically, the constellation Cassiopeia.

Exercise: Invocation to the Cosmic Mother of the Deep
Use this invocation to call upon the energies of these goddesses of the fertile waters.

> Cosmic Mother of the Deep,
> Bless me while I am awake and while I sleep.
> Mother of the stars in the sky,
> Teach me how to soar and to fly.
> Show me the limitlessness of your love
> So when I am drowning I can rise above.
> Great mother of the watery deep,
> Hold me when I smile and weep.
> Show me the mysteries of your dark water.
> Hold me as your cosmic watery daughter.

Celtic Goddess Grimoire

CHAPTER 14

Rosmerta—The Great Provider

Name variations: Rosemerta
Region: central and eastern Gaul, southwest England, Gloucester,
    Bath, Waserburg in Alsace, Baden and Trier in Germany,
    Burgundy
Sacred associations: snake, caducei, caduceus, genii cucullati,
    scepter, bucket and ladle, torch, patera, cornucopia, sacred
    springs, purse
Bodies of water: River Rhine, River Rhone, River Meuse, River
    Moselle

Rosmerta is a Celtic and Germanic abundance goddess who was also venerated by the Romans in southwest Britain and in Gaul. Many reliefs dedicated to her have been found in Celtic lands, as well as temple remains. She is linked with both the Rhine and Rhone rivers, and is associated with springs, healing, prosperity, abundance, protection, and fruitfulness. She is sometimes found holding the Cauldron of Rebirth. The Romans identified her as the consort of Mercury, while Germanic devotees considered her wed to Woden. In continental Europe, she is seen as consort to Mercury. In these cases, she seems to have become the "other half," or counterpart, of Mercury through divine marriage. In Britain, however, she stands alone and is seen as an individual with powers in her own right.

In Gallo-Roman regions, Rosmerta was worshiped as a goddess of fertility and abundance, her attributes and associations reflecting plenty. Her name, which is Gallic in origin, means "the great provider." Many statues and inscriptions to the goddess survive. One shows her seated with Mercury holding symbols of abundance like a cornucopia and a patera, or offering bowl. Another shows the couple in the same relative positions, with Rosmerta holding a purse in her right hand and a patera in her left. A pair of statues in Paris depict the couple together, with Rosmerta holding a cornucopia and a basket of fruit. In one bronze statue, the goddess appears alone sitting on a rock holding a purse, with the wings of Mercury on her head.

Twenty-seven inscriptions to Rosmerta have been found scattered across Roman provinces in France, Germany and Luxembourg, many of which refer to Mercury and the goddess jointly. This consistent pairing with the god Mercury reenforces the goddess's association with abundance. In two, she is given the epithet *sacra*, meaning "sacred." Another associates her with the dedication of a shrine where rites of hospitality were celebrated, emphasizing her attributes as the great provider and source of good fortune.

Rosmerta is the full and embodied representation of overflowing abundance. A relief in the Roman museum in Bath depicts her with a wooden bucket as the "source of plenty." Below her are the *genii cucullati*, Celtic spirits often found in groups of three. In Germany, she is depicted with a patera and a cornucopia. Some reliefs show her feeding a snake from a purse or bucket-like vessel, suggesting a possible association with the Cauldron of Rebirth.

The large number of surviving reliefs and depictions of this goddess may indicate that she was popular with the local tribes and village folk—not surprising, given her role as the bringer of abundance.

Exercise: Invocation to Rosmerta

Here is an invocation you use to call on Rosmerta's blessings.

> Rosmerta of the healing spring,
> Abundance in my life please do bring.
> Fertile goddess of the land,
> I call to you here, where I stand.
> Powerful goddess of fertile ground,
> Bestow your blessings all around.

Exercise: Abundance Ritual

This ritual can be done to honor Rosmerta, or you can modify it to honor your own matron goddess.

You will need:

- A basket that can fit on your altar or in your ritual space
- A green cloth
- A large ritual vessel or sacred bowl
- A small ritual vessel or sacred bowl
- Offerings of fruit, vegetables, and flowers
- Spring water or blessed water

Lay a green cloth on your altar or in your ritual space to attract abundance and place the larger ritual vessel in the center. Take the smaller ritual vessel and place it in the center of the larger one. Fill the larger bowl with juicy fruit, lush green leaves, ripe vegetables, and delicate and fragrant flowers. Try to use plants that are in season or that you can find in your local environment. When the contents of the larger vessel are arranged around the smaller one to your liking, pour the blessed water into the smaller vessel in the center, giving the offerings of earth and the lifeforce of water to the goddess.

Leave these bowls on your altar until the lifeforce has drained from them. When the water turns stale, gift it back to the earth, praying to Rosmerta for fertile abundance for yourself and the earth. When the fruit and vegetables begin to rot, either give them to wildlife or compost them into the earth, praying for prosperity for yourself and the land.

CHAPTER 15

Airmid—Goddess of Healing Herbs

Name variations: Airmed, Airmid
Region: Ireland
Sacred associations: healing, tears, loss, herbal plants, study of
    plants
Offerings: tears, flowers, herbal bundles, natural objects, honey,
    milk
Body of water: Well of Slaine

Airmid is an Irish goddess associated with herbal and healing knowledge. She is mentioned in *Cath Dédenach Maige Tuired*, which relates the second battle of Maige Tuired, as having helped heal wounds on the battlefield.

Irish lore tells us that Airmid and her brother Miach were raised by the divine physician Dian Cécht. When the Irish king Nuadu was wounded and deemed unfit to rule, Dian Cécht fashioned a prosthetic hand for him out of silver. (A king who had been wounded or maimed, or who had lost a limb, was considered unfit to rule.) Although the prosthetic moved just like a real hand, it remained silver. Miach was not satisfied with this and sought a way to transform the hand into actual flesh and blood. So he went to the hand and said: "Joint to joint and sinew to sinew." Then he carried the hand by his side for three days. At the end of the three days, skin had grown to cover it. Over the next three days, he carried the hand against his chest and then, for a final three days, he blackened bulrushes and cast white wisps across it, attempting to further improve it.

When Dian Cécht discovered this, he erupted in a jealous rage and threw his sword at Miach's head, cutting the flesh. But Miach had great skill as a healer and healed himself. So Dian Cécht threw his sword again, this time cutting Miach to the bone. Once again, Miach healed himself. When Dian Cécht threw his sword at Miach a third time, he cut through both flesh and bone and into his brain. Yet still Miach healed himself. Then the enraged physician finally removed Miach's brain, killing him and burying his body.

Airmid wept upon her brother's grave, her tears watering 365 medicinal flowers and herbs that grew there—the number of bones and sinews in Miach's body. As she tended to the grave, she also tended the flowers and herbs there, noticing their wide variety. So she spread out her cloak and began to pick, harvest, and uproot the plants, taking note of their medicinal properties, and studying and classifying them. One day, when her task was close to being finished, Dian Cécht crept up behind her and scattered all the herbs and flowers she had gathered and classified, thus scattering the knowledge of the healing power of herbal plants.

Here is an exercise you can use to draw upon some of this healing power.

Exercise: Healing Herbal Bundle

For this exercise, you'll be spending time in nature. If you have a garden, that is the perfect place to start. If not, pack up your supplies and take a nature walk to a local park or forest. Be sure to pick a place where you are allowed to pick fresh flowers, grasses, herbs, and other natural objects. Bring about a yard of blue thread or yarn with you. Blue is the color often associated with healing, but you can also use red. If you feel inspired to use other colors because of a particular association, feel free to do so. You may also want to bring garden shears or durable scissors.

Before you begin your walk, assemble the items that you need. Then say this quick incantation:

> As Airmid went out
> To seek medicinal herbs,
> So do I go out
> To create a healing charm.

Begin walking, looking for beautiful grasses, small branches, wildflowers, and herbs. Listen to the spirit of the plants and let them guide you.

Since you won't be using this bundle medicinally or internally, you can use any plant that you feel drawn to. If you don't know the plants in your area, I highly recommend getting a local field guide. It's always good to know which flowers and herbs dry well. Some will dry better than others. Always be cautious and know what plants like poison oak and poison ivy look like. Consider wearing gloves unless you're 100 percent sure about the plants you're harvesting. You don't want to end up with a handful of stinging nettle or hogsweed, as that could be quite uncomfortable or lead to long-term skin damage.

Take a deep breath, ground yourself, and then call on Airmid to aid you in learning about the plants. In your own words, ask her to bring her healing energy to the charm. Each time you take a piece of a plant, be sure that you leave plenty for next season. Leave an offering of honey, milk, or a taglock like a piece of your hair. Give one of these as an offering to the earth once you have gathered three, six, or nine different plants.

Sit down holding the plants in your hands and speak to the spirit of each plant. Lay out the plants as you feel led, bundling them together in a way that is pleasing to you. When you are happy with the bundle, begin wrapping the blue or other colored thread around it. Do this at least nine times, being sure to pull the thread tight and tie it each time. As you tie the first knot, say:

Bone to bone.

As you tie the second knot, say:

Vein to vein.

As you tie the third knot, say:

Balm to balm.

As you tie the fourth knot, say:

Sap to sap.

As you tie the fifth knot, say:

Skin to skin.

As you tie the sixth knot, say:

Tissue to tissue.

As you tie the seventh knot, say:

   Blood to blood.

As you tie the eighth knot, say:

   Flesh to flesh.

As you tie the ninth knot, say:

   Sinew to sinew.

When all nine knots are tied, say:

   Airmid, of the herbs,
   Healer of healers,
   May I be an isle in the sea,
   May I be a hill on the shore,
   May I be a star in waning of the moon,
   May I be a staff to the weak.
   As these magical plants heal,
   Gracious Airmid,
   May I heal and be healed.

When you are finished, tie a bow and carry the bundle back to your home altar and leave it there for at least one night. The next morning, examine it and make any adjustments you may need. You can remove the thread and rebind it now that the plants have had an opportunity to dry a little, but be sure to say the charm again as you do. Sprinkle any blessed water that you have on hand and hang the bundle near your bed.

PART IV

Goddesses of Battle and Justice

CHAPTER 16

Andraste—Invincible Goddess of War

Name variations: Andte, may be connected to Andarta
Region: England, specifically modern-day Norfolk
Sacred associations: victory, war, resisting masculine oppression, reclaiming power, leadership, divination, chariot, hare
Offerings: weapons, coins, shields, food offerings, activism
Body of water: none

Andraste is a battle goddess worshiped by the Iceni, a tribe who lived in eastern Britain during the Iron Age and the early Roman era. Their most famous queen, Boudica, was a legendary warrior queen whose name derives from *bouda*, which means "victory." Very little is known about the goddess Andraste, but much that we do know has survived through the story of Boudica, who is considered perhaps the greatest warrior queen in British history. While Boudica was not considered a goddess, she is revered as an ancestral figure from whom we can still learn great lessons. Although she was given the title of consort, which legitimized her rule after the death of her husband, Prasutagus, she is referred to in the surviving record as Queen Boudica, and is just as important as the Celtic warrior queen Cartimandua of the Brigantes.

Boudica is important to our understanding of Andraste because she gives us insight into the fierce power that Celtic women held. Celtic women were considered equal to their male counterparts. They were educated and understood their value in society. When the Romans invaded Celtic lands, many local rulers made deals with them in order to retain their power. In the case of Prasutagus, he agreed to submit to the Romans provided that he could keep his lands for his lifetime. Boudica rejected this agreement, however, because, as an equal in Celtic society, she would inherit those lands along with her daughters. When the Romans came to claim her husband's property after his death, she refused to give up what was rightfully hers. The Romans took her lands by force, bound her and whipped her publicly, and assaulted her daughters.

In her rage at this horrific treatment, this fierce queen fomented an uprising that soon soaked the disputed lands in the blood of Roman legions. She raised an army of more than 120,000 and slaughtered the Ninth Legion. Before the battle began, Boudica called upon Andraste in a ferocious speech, then performed a divination ritual that gave an auspicious result and indicated victory. The record shows that the Celtic forces under Boudica's command destroyed close to 70,000 Romans. Moreover, she succeeded in completely humiliating the Roman legions by defeating them with an army led by a woman. Her victory did not last long, however, and the Romans sent other legions in support of the Ninth, eventually defeating the Celts. It is said that Boudica committed suicide after the defeat rather than be captured by the Romans once again.

Women as battle commanders were common in the Celtic world, and this is where we find the link to Andraste. In fact, we can learn much about Andraste from Boudica, and much about ourselves as well. They both remind us that we do not have to submit to unfair rule. We do not have to submit to false patriarchal constructs. We do not have to give up our land, our sovereignty, our bodies, or our souls to anyone. They teach us how to rise up in the face of evil and oppression and defeat them. Thus Andraste is the perfect goddess to call upon when we wage war on capitalism, oppression, and the patriarchy.

Andraste, although little is known about her directly, is associated with victory through her link with Boudica. She is a warrior goddess for women, but also for all people, as Boudica was a warrior queen for all Celts. Together they teach us how to turn rage into paradigm-shifting actions. From them, we learn to stand in sovereignty, even when our legs are shaking. From them, we learn how to push past fear and trust in the ferocity of our own spirits. We see that we are powerful beyond measure and that, when we stand united, we can achieve victory over our oppressors. Together, Andraste and Boudica teach us to value victory over retreat, courage over fear. They give us the fortitude to reclaim our power from those who seek to control us.

Exercise: Prayer for Victory

Use this prayer when you feel threatened by the forces of oppression, or when you feel the need to reclaim your power as a woman.

> Andraste, I pray for your aid.
> Warrior goddess, show me the way to victory.
> Show me how Boudica held her army strong
> And how she stood in the face of all that she knew was wrong.
> May I find victory in all that I do
> And may her fierceness and power run through me.
> And if I do not prevail in my quest for a fair and righteous world,
> Then let my daughters and their daughters find their fierceness in the tale of my own journey.
> May my children find strength in knowing that their mother was strong.
> Let the fire burning a hole in my chest burn bright for the young girls yet to come.
> May my story inspire greatness in them as Boudica's did in me.
> May I be so fierce, so powerful, and so strong that my story lasts for eons.
> May it ripple out through time to strengthen girls yet to come.
> Let the beating of my courageous heart be a drumbeat for future generations.
> May they summon my spirit from the ancestral realms to strengthen them in their own battles.
> May women rise again and again with the strength of Boudica.
> Oh Andraste, warrior divine, weave my story now.
> Show me where I am fierce, where I am bold, where I can change the world.
> May every battle scar become the armor by which you strengthen me.
> May my failures be lessons and my triumphs change the world.

Exercise: Invocation to Andraste and Boudica

Use this invocation to call upon the fierceness and power of Andraste, the warrior goddess, and Boudica, the warrior queen, when you feel need for them in your life.

Goddess Andraste and Boudica Queen,
I call you forth from the realms unseen.
Goddess of victory, goddess of might,
I seek your favor on this dark night.
Bring forth your victory in this potent hour.
Andraste, I implore your ferocious power.

Exercise: Divination Disk

This exercise is adapted from the ritual that Boudica is reported to have performed before her battle with the Romans, in which she let a hare loose from under her skirts to divine the outcome of the battle. While we can't do this in the modern world, we can use the imagery of the story to create a divination tool that connects us with Andraste through this iconic queen.

In this exercise, you will create a divination disk that you can use to receive simple "Yes" and "No" answers. While this may seem overly simple, divination rituals like this have been used for thousands of years and are still used in practices like a simple coin toss. Use these answers to check your intuition, or to divine if an offering or ritual is in alignment before you do the working. They can also help you differentiate between authentic messages from spirit and messages from ego that may be clouding your judgment.

You will need:

- A round wooden disk an inch and a half to two inches across. You can find these at craft stores and they are usually very affordable. You can also use a disk cut from a branch if it is the right size. Leave the bark on if you do, as this will give it a nice touch.
- Painted or cut paper images
- Mod podge

On one side of the disk, place an image of a hare in motion. Leave the other side blank or put an image of a little hare burrow on it to indicate that the hare is staying hidden or is obscured from view. Charge the disk with your intent in this two-part ritual.

On a Full Moon, place the disk on your altar with the hare facing up. Dip your finger in some freshly created silvered water (see chapter 10) and draw a triskele on the disk. Place your hands over the disk and visualize the spirals spinning in a sunwise motion, while saying:

> By Full Moon and sacred hare,
> I employ this disk to reveal secrets to me.
> Help me to become aware
> Of what the spirits wish me to see.
> When the hare is revealed,
> A forward fate is sealed.
> This is my will, so mote it be!

On the dark of the moon, gather some fine dirt or sand from the land where you live. Return to your altar and flip the disk over showing the blank or burrow side. Sprinkle the dirt on top of the disk, saying:

> By the dark night and obscured moon,
> I employ this disk to reveal secrets to me.
> Help me to become aware
> Of what the spirits wish me to see.
> When the hare is hidden,
> Forward motion is forbidden.
> This is my will, so mote it be!

Now your disk is ready to use.

Speak the incantation below before tossing the disk to divine the answers you seek:

> Sacred goddess of the land,
> Please guide my divining hand.
> Help me to become aware,
> Of what you wish me to see.
> Andraste, please hear my plea!
> I humbly ask for you to answer me!

CHAPTER 17
The Morrigan—Phantom Queen

Name variations: Battle Fury, Morrígu, Great Queen
Region: Ireland
Sacred associations: battle, victory, prophecy, promiscuity, fecundity,
   crows, sovereignty
Offerings: crow feathers, activism, weapons
Body of water: River Unius

The Morrigan is a goddess who is deeply layered and dynamic, and it can take some time and effort to understand just who and what she is. In fact, it took me a long time to understand her completely and, to be honest, sometimes I feel as if I still don't! There comes a moment upon the path of magic and spirituality when most of us come across a force that knocks us over and leaves us stunned by the sheer intensity of what we just experienced. And I can say that The Morrigan was one of these forces for me.

If you are called to honor or work with The Morrigan, I highly recommend first learning about her through the scholarship of her devotees and practitioners. We are lucky to have the work of several amazing priestesses and devotees who have written entire books on this complex goddess. I suggest that you seek out several of these and read them before you dive deeper into a relationship with this goddess. Her devotees often describe her as fierce, intense, and sometimes downright frightening. She is not a goddess of light and love, but if you choose to honor her, she will shape and transform you into a person of strength and fortitude.

The Morrigan is a triune goddess who is both singular and made up of the three figures of Nemhain, Macha, and Babd. She is a goddess who can be seen in a triple aspect—although not as the popular trio of maiden, mother, and crone. Nemhain is an Irish war goddess whose name means "frenzy." She was known to induce panic and fear, and to incite warriors to savage battle. Babd is a war goddess who takes the form of a crow and was known to turn the tide of battle to her favored side. She sometimes appeared prior to a battle to foreshadow its outcome, and sometimes foretold a death through her wailing cries, which led to her associations with the *bean-sidhe*, or *banshees*—faery folk who presided over river fords and other liminal places that served as bridges to the Otherworld.

Macha, the third figure in this triplicity, was an Irish sovereignty goddess associated with the land, fertility, rulership, war, and fecundity (see chapter 28). She was invoked as a great queen and battle maven. The Morrigan, as a triune goddess, combines all these disparate aspects into a single deity, so it is no wonder that she is such a complicated and layered figure.

The Morrigan is known to her devotees primarily as a goddess of war and battle, but also as a goddess of destruction and fertility. She is often described as a fearsome and terrible phantom queen, but she is affectionately called the Great Queen by others. She is the patron goddess of many who serve in uniform and of those who walk the path of a warrior in service to something greater than themselves. If The Morrigan in her many guises reaches out to you, you are being called to stormy shores that lead to conflict, and you must prepare to navigate the battlefield before you. She is the power that helps you rise up against villains and oppressors. She is the swift sword and spear of justice. She is the terrifying Phantom Queen, but don't demonize her powers, because, through her actions, righteousness and justice are served.

Today, many are devoted to The Morrigan. She is a popular goddess for those who work social-justice magic and for those making change in governmental structures across the world. She is also a guide for those who work the magic of the old ways, traversing the labyrinth of the Celtic Otherworld. Her main lesson is the importance of justice.

Exercise: Candle Spell for Justice
One of The Morrigan's key attributes is the fight for justice. Try using this exercise the next time you find yourself fighting for justice in the world, or in your own life.

For this exercise, you will need:

- 3 black candles
- A tool to inscribe a candle
- River water or storm water
- 3 crow or raven feathers
- A black bowl
- Sand

Place the black bowl on your altar and fill it three quarters full with sand. Take the first candle and write the name of one aspect of The Morrigan on it, then do this for the second and third candles. Anoint your candles with river water or storm water, being sure not to get the wicks wet, then place them in the center of the bowl, pushing them down into the sand.

Take one feather and use the quill to write the word "Justice" in the sand in front of one candle, then place it in front of the bowl with the quill touching the bowl and the feather pointing away from the candles. Do this with the other two feathers, naming the second and third aspects you have chosen. When you are finished, each of the three feathers should be aligned with a candle bearing the name of an aspect of The Morrigan in the center, creating a triskele.

When you are ready, place your hands over the spell bowl and charge it with your intent. You may wish to speak your intent aloud or you can just visualize it. Then invoke The Morrigan by each of the three aspects you have chosen, being very clear to call upon her by each name. As you say each of her names, light the corresponding candle. Invoke her by using the invocation below, then speak to her directly in your own words, telling her the situation and asking her to bring justice to it. Let the candles burn down naturally, then recycle the sand or return it to where you gathered it and clean up the rest of your ingredients.

Exercise: Invocation for Justice

This invocation is based on one found in the *Carmina Gadelica*.

> I will go in the name of The Morrigan,
> In the likeness of a deer, in the likeness of a horse,
> In the likeness of a serpent, in the likeness of my Great Queen.
> Stronger am I than all others.
> The hand of The Morrigan keeps me,
> The fierceness of her is in my veins.
> The strength of her spirit washes over me.

The Three shield and aid me.
The hand of The Morrigan guides me.
In triplicate, with each step, she aids me.

Exercise: Invoking the Sword of Justice
When you need to invoke the sword of justice in your magical work or when you are involved in legal proceedings, make copies of important documents associated with your struggle. Place them in a cauldron with rosemary, blackthorn thorns, rose thorns, hawthorn thorns, rue, bay, and mugwort. Burn these until you have a substantial amount of ash. When it is cool, split the ash into three parts. Place one part of the ash mixture into a black cotton bag and seal it with a red thread. Carry this bag with you during court proceedings, when addressing legal matters, or when in need of protection.

Mix another part of the mixture with water from a ferociously flowing river, preferably a river that is associated with The Morrigan. If you don't have access to river water, use storm water instead. Then anoint any magical tools you use to work for justice or to seek The Morrigan's blessing. Use the third part of the ash to draw a sword on your inner forearms when you need to invoke the sword of justice in your magical work.

PART V
Faery Women

CHAPTER 18

Áine—The Bright One

Name variations: Áine of Knockainy, Áine Chlair, Enya
Region: Lough Gur, Limerick, Ireland
Sacred associations: bees, summer, sunbeams, red mare
Offerings: flowers, milk, honey, sun imagery, golden beryl
Body of water: Tobar Áine aka Tullaghan Well

Áine is considered a goddess of summer and plenty, and is connected to the sun. In fact, her name means "splendor," "bright," or "brightness." Her feast day is celebrated on Midsummer's Eve and her sacred associations include a red mare, sunbeams, god's eye, gold, summer, and bees.

There are several figures known as Áine. But the faery woman known by this name, Áine of Limerick, is, like other faery women, most likely a diminished version of a goddess. She may also be connected with the sun goddess Grian, who was her sister.

Áine can shapeshift into the unbeatable red mare, Lair Derg, giving her a connection to horse goddesses as well, and perhaps even another association with the sun. To anchor her even more firmly into this connection, her feast day falls on the summer solstice, and is sometimes connected with Lughnasa, which falls on August 1. Both have significant associations with the sun, as they occur during the hottest part of the year when the sun shines down and brings forth the fertility of the land.

Áine often appears in the guise of a faery maiden and is associated with Knock Áine, a faery hill in Limerick, as well as with Lough Gur, a lake in County Limerick. She, like Danu, is associated with the mountains near Killarney sometimes called the Paps of Anu or the Paps of Áine. Áine was known to have many lovers, connecting her with fertility and love. These include Mananan Mac Lir and Maurice, the earl of Desmon, who is said to have stolen her cloak. This may connect her to the folktale of the swan maiden. She may also be associated with torches and is sometimes referred to as Áine Clair.

Exercise: Invocation to Áine
Use this invocation to call on the power and blessings of this bright goddess.

> Faery queen of the solar light,
> Shine down upon me with your magical might.
> Come forth, beautiful radiant one.
> Bless me with your powers of the sun.
> Beautiful solar queen, heal me with your solar rays.
> Show me the magic of your faery rays.
> Red Mare, with splendor bright,
> Illuminate me with your blessed light.

Exercise: Charmed Water for Luck
For this exercise, you will need a golden or yellow beryl, a crystal that occurs naturally in Ireland and is called the "gift from the sun."

Place a golden or yellow beryl in a clear bowl filled with spring water, then add three shamrocks and the petals from calendula flowers. Let the water sit in the sun for three hours, then use it to anoint candles, your body, or your Good Fortune Bee Bag (see below). You can also add it to a bath or use it in other magical workings, or give it as an offering to Áine. If you want to ingest the water, be sure to place the beryl in a clear glass jar and then place that in the bowl ensuring that the water does not touch the crystal, which contains aluminum.

Exercise: Good Fortune Bee Bag
Celts in old Devonshire often kept bees in pouches and hung them in the home to bring good fortune, health, and happiness. Here's a simple charm bag you can make to bring these blessings into your life.

You will need:

- A green pouch or bag
- 3 to 9 dried bees

Bees have a very short life span and can often be found in fields, in the blossoms of flowers, or near hives, so there's no need to risk getting stung by trying to harvest a live bee. And you should avoid killing any precious bees who are pollinating our flowers. It may be easier to find dried bees in late summer to early fall when they die off naturally.

When you have collected your bees, place them in a green pouch or bag and carry them with you for good fortune.

Exercise: Faery Queen Sun Tea

Here's a simple tea you can make to connect you to the faery realms. You will need:

- Dried chamomile
- Dried hawthorn flowers
- Dried calendula flowers
- Dried yarrow flowers
- Fresh or dried rose (preferably yellow or orange)
- 3 to 6 bags of your favorite tea

Place these in a large clear jar or jug and cover with spring water. Then place the container ourside in the early morning and leave it for six to nine hours in direct sunlight. When the tea is ready, strain all the flowers out with a wire mesh strainer and add honey to your taste. Then relax, sip your tea, and enjoy.

CHAPTER 19
Nicnevin—Faery Queen

Name variations: McNevin, Queen of the Faeries
Region: Scotland
Sacred associations: magic wand, yarn, weaving, divination,
    nymphs, witchcraft
Offerings: hawthorn crown, milk and honey, bowls of spring water
Body of water: the sea

Nicnevin is a Scottish faery woman who may have links to the goddess
Nemain and is sometimes linked to The Cailleach. Nicnevin is also sometimes seen as a witch or a supernatural being called the Gyre-Carline. Her
name may mean "destroying," but it is more widely believed to mean "daughter of Nevis," which connects her with her home in Ben Nevis. She also
seems to have a watery connection, and it is said that she can command
nymphs and has the ability to change rocks into water, as well as the power
to reshape the landscape. She is sometimes described as a faery queen, and
is sometimes depicted as a witch or a hag wearing a gray cloak.

There is very little known about Nicnevin, who is first mentioned in
"The Flyting of Montgomery," a poem from the late 1500s. Here, she is
described as one of a large number of nymphs who carry charms and whose
magical workings included casting a "clew," or a ball of yarn, indicating an
association with spinners and weavers of magic.

Nicneuen with her nymphes, in number anew,
With charmes from Caitnes and Chanrie of Rosse,
Whose cunning consists in casting of a Clew.

She may also be associated with trance work via spinning, since the choice of the word "casting" may indicate that a type of divination or trance work was taking place.

Centuries later, Sir Walter Scott also mentions Nicnevin, but characterizes her as a witch and a giantess, which associates her more closely with The Cailleach in her aspect as hag. And, in fact, McNevin, one variation of her name, is sometimes conflated with the Gyre-Carling, a witch or oger-like figure, and with Hecate. Since The Cailleach is also sometimes referred to as the Gyre-Carling, this tends to reenforce their connection. Mothers frequently frightened their children by threatening to give them to McNevin or to the Gyre-Carling, who is described as wearing a long gray mantle and carrying a wand that could convert water into rocks and the sea into dry land.

Exercise: Hawthorn Crown

On Beltane or in honor of these faery women, craft a crown out of hawthorn and place it at the base of a hawthorn tree or on your altar. Place candles around it and adorn it with other contrasting flowers, pretty leaves, interesting stones, crystals, and pieces of bark. In the center, place a small dish with offerings of milk, honey, and delicate scented fresh flower petals.

Exercise: Tangle of Thorns Binding Spell

This is a simple spell that can be very effective. The most important ingredient is a taglock of a person you want to bind or trap in a web of their own lies. Hair is ideal, but if you don't have access to this, use a picture or the person's name and birthdate written on a very thin sliver of paper.

For this exercise, you will need:

- Several rose canes with a thorny stem (a hawthorn branch, blackthorn, or blackberry vine will also work)
- Gloves to protect your hands
- Thread or yarn (I usually choose a red thread, but use your intuition)
- A taglock of the person you want to bind

On the dark or waning moon, gather your thorns and begin weaving them together. Be sure that the paper or hair taglock is woven into the thorns as you do this. Then, starting at the top, wind the thread or yarn toward the bottom of the thorn bundle in a counterclockwise direction. When you are done, bring the two ends of the thread together and tie six knots in it to seal the spell. Then sprinkle storm water on the bundle of thorns. As you do this, see the person you have bound become stuck in the thorns. With each lie they tell, the thorns dig deeper into their skin. Each time they try to harm you, the same thing happens. Bury this bundle at the base of a thorny bush.

Exercise: Meeting the Faery Queen

Begin by finding a comfortable place to relax—outside near a hawthorn tree if you can, but another type of tree will work as well. If you don't have access to a quiet place outside, do this at your altar or in your sacred space.

Relax, settle in, and close your eyes. Let go of the thoughts and worries of the day and let your mind become clear and your body grounded. Focus on your breath. Begin to breathe rhythmically, focusing on the sensations of the air moving in and out of your lungs. Feel your connection to the earth beneath you and to the sacred trees around you. Be present in this moment.

In your mind's eye, visualize nothing and hear only the sounds of nature. Don't let any thoughts intrude. Focus on the darkness around you. You see a small sliver of light in front of you and move toward it, not quite understanding what it is. As you get closer, the light illuminates more of the space around you, and you can see a large wooden door with a wooden handle. The sliver of light comes from a crack in this door. You approach the door and put your hand on the handle. You gently push open the door.

You find yourself standing in the doorway of a small cottage at the edge of a village with warm yellow lights glowing in the windows. You pass through the village until you reach a tiny little house at the end of the path. You climb three steps and move onto a cobblestone roadway. Turning away from the village, you begin to walk down the road.

You can hear frogs croaking and a rustling in the bushes nearby. The sun begins to set, leaving your view obscured. A light gray mist begins to form all around you. After walking for some time, you reach the end of the path, where you find a large hedge full of thorns and berries. Unafraid, you reach toward the hedge and, finding firm handholds, begin to climb up it, putting your feet on one branch and then another, then another. You feel your clothing being tugged by the thorns and, as you reach the top, you feel a sharp prick in your finger and see three drops of blood fall onto the top of the hedge, a clear sacrifice for crossing the hedge. Each becomes a red berry.

You swing your legs over the top of the hedge and begin to descend down the other side, moving with much more ease than you did on your climb up it. In front of you, you see a field of wildflowers and tall grasses. You move through it across the landscape, until you come upon a mound where a hawthorn tree grows. The tree is in full bloom, with white flowers covering it and tiny white petals falling like snowdrops to the ground. You look down at your wrist and see a small braided cord made of red, white, and black thread. You untie it and whisper a blessing, then gently tie it to the tree. Then you kneel down and see a small stone altar with a simple bowl of honey and a pitcher of milk on it. You pour the milk along the roots of the tree. Then you dip your fingers into the honey and draw a seven-pointed star, the faery star, on the stone (see Figure 12).

Figure 12. The seven-pointed faery star.

You sit beneath the hawthorn tree and close your eyes. The sweet smell of the honey and hawthorn blossoms fills your nostrils, the sound of bees buzzing to and from each flower fills your ears, and the sensation of a light breeze moves across your skin. Petals from the hawthorn tree kiss your cheeks.

A bright shining light appears in front of you. You take a deep breath and bask in the beauty and majesty of the shining one you see—a most powerful Otherworldly faery queen clothed all in white, with long hair and a magical form. You stand and she gently takes your hand and places it on the trunk of the tree. She tells you to listen—to listen to the wisdom of the greenwood, to listen to the heartbeat of the land. She invites you to share the wisdom of the Otherworld and the wisdom the faery folk. She asks why you seek her and what you hope to find in the faery realm. You take a moment to speak with her and learn her wisdom.

When you are finished communing with the beautiful shining faery queen, you bid her farewell. Once again, you feel the hawthorn petals falling from the tree above kiss your cheeks. You blink a few times and realize that you've been dreaming. You descend the mound and leave the tree behind, moving back through the field of flowers, back across the field of tall grasses, weaving in and out back toward the hedge—the boundary between this world and the Otherworld.

As you get closer to the hedge, you notice that the three drops of your blood have turned from berries into flowers—three crimson-red hawthorn flowers clustered among the white flowers of the hedge. You quickly climb the hedge and cross back over the boundary to the safety of the village, moving back up the cobblestone path. With only the moon to guide you, you find your way back to the little cottage at the edge of the village and push open the door. You step through and close the door behind you. As you push the door closed, the sliver of light that shone through it fades, leaving you in darkness.

In the silence and darkness, bring your focus back to your breath, allowing the air to slowly fill your lungs. Feel the expansion of your rib cage as you inhale, and its relaxing as you exhale. Bring your attention to your fingers and toes, and give them a quick squeeze. Then gently allow your head to move from side to side. When you're ready, bring your awareness back to this time and this space.

CHAPTER 20

Ladies of the Lake

One of the most famous representations of the Celtic Divine Feminine is found in Arthurian lore in the story of Nimue, the Lady of the Lake. When you think of the Lady of the Lake, no doubt your mind takes you to this legend. While this is accurate, it is not even close to the full picture. There isn't just one single Lady of the Lake. Rather, there are many ladies associated with various bodies of water. In the Welsh tradition, these lake maidens are called Gwragedd Annwn. Cows are considered sacred to them and are found in various stories of magic related to these watery women.

Some of these magical lake ladies' names include Viviane, Elaine, Niniane, Nivian, Nineveh, or Evienne. Nimue is probably the most popular of them, but, as with many other faery women, there are different versions of her story. She is sometimes described as Merlin's beloved, and sometimes she is conflated with Morgause.

But the original Lady of the Lake comes from a story in *The Mabinogi*, and this should not be confused with the Arthurian tale. There are also several other versions of this original story, and I have combined key elements of the original with later folktales to create the story below.

THE LADY OF LLYN Y FAN FACH

Name variations: The Lady of Llyn y Fan Fach
Region: Brecon Beacons, Wales
Sacred associations: herbs, cows, lakes, the number three
Offerings: herbs, lake water, fresh cow's milk, bread
Body of water: Llyn y Fan Fach

The story of the Lady of Llyn y Fan Fach begins with a young man who was walking one day through the hills of Wales, leading his herd of sheep to the fields to graze. When he stopped near a lake to rest, he saw a beautiful young maiden emerge from the water. She waved to him and asked to share his bread. He complied and she thanked him, but said that the bread was too soft and asked if he could bring her some harder bread the next day. He agreed and, that night, his mother helped him bake a harder loaf.

The next day, the young man brought the bread to the lake. Once again, the beautiful maiden emerged from the water, and once again the young man shared his bread with her. This time, however, she thought the bread was too hard and asked if he could bring her bread that was not too soft and not too hard. He agreed and, once again, went home to bake her bread.

The following day, the young man returned to the lake with the bread and the maiden tasted it. Happy that it was neither too soft nor too hard, she said that she would marry him on one condition—that if he ever struck her three times, she would leave him. Knowing that he could never harm such a beautiful and sweet creature, he instantly agreed. She told him to come back the next day and they would marry.

When he returned the next day, an old man emerged from the lake accompanied by two girls who were identical in every way, even to their clothing. The old man said that if the young man could tell which one had shared his bread, he could marry her. When he could not decide between the two, one maiden slipped her foot forward just a bit and he noticed the small movement. He chose her and they were soon wed. The young maiden brought with her a large dowry of cows that rose out of the lake one by one.

As time passed, the couple had three lovely sons. One day, as they were leaving for a wedding, the wife realized that she had forgotten her gloves and asked her husband to get them. He agreed, but said that he hadn't hitched the horses to the cart yet and asked if she would do it for him so they wouldn't be late. She said yes, but when he returned with her gloves, he found she had not even begun. When, in frustration, he lightly tapped her with the gloves, she turned to him and said: "You have now struck me once. If you strike me twice more, I will leave you." Clearly upset, the husband hitched the horses himself and they set off for the wedding.

When at the wedding, the wife suddenly began to cry in the middle of the ceremony. The husband, confused and frustrated, patted her several times on the arm trying to calm her. She then turned to him and said: "You have now struck me twice. If you ever strike me again, I will leave you." *Afraid that he would lose his beautiful wife, the man took great care not to strike her again.*

After a time, someone in the village passed away and the couple decided to attend the funeral. As they were paying their respects, the wife suddenly began to laugh hysterically. Once again, surprised by her reaction and frustrated, her husband tapped her arm trying to quiet her. She turned to him with deep sadness in her eyes and said: "You have now struck me three times." She stood up and walked back to the lake, disappearing into the water. Then all the cows she had brought as her dowry followed her into the water, along with their offspring.

The Lady of Llyn y Fan Fach emerged every so often to spend time with her sons and to teach them the mystery of the healing arts. Her sons carried her knowledge forward, passing it down to the next generation. They eventually became the most famous physicians in Wales—the physicians of Myddfai, whose line can be traced all the way back to the late 1800s.

The main lesson of this watery maiden is that we must ask for what we want. From her, we learn personal sovereignty, boundary-setting, healing from abuse, and the need to stick up for ourselves and walk away from bad situations.

Exercise: Bread of Sovereignty
In this exercise, you will make bread. Choose your favorite dough recipe and make any adjustments you want to it—like using gluten-free flour or vegan alternatives for eggs and butter. You will also need some thyme, rosemary, garlic, basil, oregano, sage, and butter.

Prepare your dough and split it into three sections. Butter three small bread pans and place a third of the dough in each. Mix the herbs with a little salt and three tablespoons of melted butter, then brush the butter mixture onto the bread. Place all three pans in the oven together and set the timer for ten minutes before the loaves are supposed to be done. When the timer goes off, take one loaf out of the oven so that it is undercooked. Remove the second loaf when it is done, leaving the third loaf in the oven until it becomes overbaked and hard. Then remove it as well.

Place all three loaves on your altar. Take the underbaked bread in your hands and enter into a light meditative or trance state. Begin to contemplate your life, letting your mind lead you. Do you focus on the spiritual? On the physical? On the emotional aspects of yourself? As you hold the soft bread, try to determine where you are too soft in your own life path. Where have you "underbaked" yourself? Where have you let others stomp on you? How did you suffer by being too soft and how can you change that in the future? Then place the bread back on the altar.

Next, take the overbaked bread and hold it as you contemplate where you have been too hard. Where have you met yourself or others with harshness? How did that hinder your own progress? How does being too hard and rigid affect you and how can you rise above it in the future? When you are done, place the loaf back on the altar.

Finally, pick up the bread that is perfectly cooked, neither too hard nor too soft. This loaf embodies a balance between hardness and softness. What can you learn from this? How can you seek that balance in your life? What does your "perfect loaf" look like and feel like to you? What can you learn from this? When you are finished, replace the loaf on the altar.

Cut the perfectly cooked loaf into slices and eat one slice. As you enjoy the bread, contemplate balance and how it can be such an important part of healing. Commune with the Lady of Llyn y Fan Fach and seek her wisdom. When you are finished, gift her the rest of the perfectly baked bread. Take the loaves that are too hard and too soft and gift them to the earth or to wildlife.

CHAPTER 21

Morgan le Fae—Magician and Healer

Name variations: Morgan le fae, Morganna, Modron
Region: England, Wales, Cornwall
Sacred associations: sea, sacred wells, magic, healing, shapeshifting,
  herbal arts
Offerings: apples, roses, shells, sea water, lake water, hawthorn,
  spring water
Bodies of water: the sea, the lake marshes of Avalon, Modron's
  Well, Red and White Springs in Glastonbury

Morgan le Fae is first mentioned in the *Vita Merlini,* where she is described as a benevolent shapeshifter, a healer, and the ruler of Avalon. She has assumed many different roles across time and in Arthurian tales, but is first known for her skill in the herbal arts and in the making of ointments and potions. It was only in the 13th century, in what is known as the "Vulgate Cycle," that she was demonized and turned into the evil sorceress and half-sister of King Arthur. Unfortunately, it is this portrayal of her that we so often see on television and in films.

But Morgan le Fae is much more than the antagonizing half-sister of King Arthur. She is an enchantress, a healer, and a shapeshifter who is strongly connected to the faery realm. Her name means "sea born," indicating that she may have been born of the sea and connecting her to sacred waters. Many believe that the name Morgan is a title rather than her name, while others believe that she is one of the Mari-Morgans, Welsh and Breton water spirits. There is also a group of Welsh water fae called the Gwragedd Annwn who live at the bottom of lakes, tend gardens, and have healing skills—clearly early representations of the Lady of the Lake and another possible connection with the faery realm. Gwragedd Annwn in fact means "wife of the underworld." When King Arthur is mortally wounded, Morgan le Fae escorts him to Avalon to be healed. Avalon is sometimes considered the Otherworld, and this could very well be where she gets her underworld connection.

In the *Vita Merlini*, Morgan is named as the chief of nine sisters who preside over Avalon, a wild untamed place that is also known as "the Fortunate Isle" because it produces its own grain, apple trees, grapes, and other crops. She is acknowledged as being incredibly intelligent and skilled as an herbalist and healer. She is credited with teaching her sisters mathematics and is known to have the ability to shapeshift.

Morgan is another mysterious goddess figure. There are many references to her throughout the historical record that have left us with a fragmented picture of who she was. She is described as a faery woman, but many believe—and modern scholarship supports—that Morgan is a derivation of a mother goddess, Modron, who is the daughter of Affalach and associated with Ynys Affalach, a possible Welsh derivation of the Isle of Avalon. Some argue, however, that this etymology only arose during the medieval period, and that it is more likely that the term *affalach* refers to apples or apple trees. This, they claim, is the origin of Morgan's connection to Avalon. There is also mention of Affalach being the King of Annwn, another form of the Welsh underworld, connecting Morgan le Fae with that realm and with another group of nine women known as the Nine Maidens of Annwn (see chapter 22).

When Morgan le Fae is first mentioned in the Vita Merlini, she is considered a benevolent being with hints of her faery-like nature. But Gerald of Wales describes her as a faery goddess. In another text, *Sir Gawain and the Green Knight*, she is described as "Morgan the Goddess." Later, however, she is demonized and her benevolent nature almost disappears as she becomes the villain of the Arthurian tales. Scholars who have traced Morgan le Fae back through history, however, believe that she is most closely related to Modron, a mother goddess whose sacred spring is in Cornwall. Modron, whose name means "mother," appears briefly in *The Mabinogi*, where she is identified as the mother of Mabon. These discrepancies reenforce Morgan's role as a shapeshifter and, although there is much debate about which story gives a more accurate picture of this enigmatic figure, it is very apparent that she has the ability to change, to adapt, and to evolve through literature and over time.

Morgan le Fae is often confused with The Morrigan, probably because of their similar names. However, it is important to note and understand that Morgan le Fae is not the same as the Irish goddess. She is a mysterious figure who is most popular in her form as a faery woman, a healer, a sorceress, and an enchantress. In fact, she is more closely linked to Modron and the Matronae than she is to the Irish Morrigan.

Today, Morgan Le Fae is featured in many movies, television shows, and comic books, and her spirit is alive and well in Glastonbury, where many believe that Avalon was located. Many of her worshipers make pilgrimages to Glastonbury to spend time in the sacred waters and on the sacred lands, walking through the groves of apple trees. It is here, in modern-day Glastonbury, that many come to seek healing and to partake of the sacred waters of the Red and White Springs.

Exercise: Healing Ointment
You can draw on the healing powers of Morgan by creating this healing ointment.

For this exercise, you will need:

- 16-ounce jar with a lid
- 6 to 8 ounces of carrier oil (almond or jojoba are recommended)
- Small tins or jars to pour the wax into
- ½ to 1 ounce bee's wax
- Oil
- Dried roses
- Dried hawthorn flowers
- Dried calendula
- Dried comfrey
- Dried yarrow
- Dried lavender
- Fine mesh wire strainer
- Double-boiler
- Rosemary oil

Begin by placing the herbs into the jar, layering them evenly until they fill it about one half to three quarters full. Fill the rest of the jar with the carrier oil, leaving a little room at the top. Stir the mixture until all the dried herbs are covered and soaked, then cap the jar tightly and place it on your altar. Let it sit for nine weeks, shaking it each day and turning the jar to mix the herbs and the oil.

Figure 13. Dolmen stone at Saint Materiana's Church in Tintagel, often named as the birthplace of King Arthur and the location of Merlin's Cave. Today, this place is sometimes associated with Morgan le Fae.

When it is ready, use the wire strainer to remove the herbs, being sure to get every drop of oil you can. Pour the infused herbal oil into the top of a double-boiler with water in the bottom and place over a low heat. Add the bee's wax and stir it until it is melted. Test the consistency with a spoon by dipping it in and allowing it to cool. Add more bee's wax until the ointment is the consistency you prefer. Once you are satisfied, add nine drops of rosemary oil and pour the mixture into the smaller tins or jars.

Exercise: Apple Spell for Healing

This spell connects to Morgan's power through the magic of apples.

For this exercise, you will need:

- A boline, or white-handled or crescent-shaped knife
- A jar to collect water
- A black candle
- Sea water
- A red apple
- A lighter

To begin, visit the ocean at low tide. Walk to the water's edge and count nine waves. When the ninth wave comes toward you, collect the water. If you do not live near the ocean, you can use water from a spring or river. In this case, dip your jar into the water nine times, making sure it is full on the ninth dip.

Bring the water home and place it on your altar. When you are ready to do the spell, cut a small hole in the top of the apple just large enough to hold the black candle. Next, carve the symbol of the vesica piscis—a shape associated with modern-day Avalon and the Divine Feminine—on the front of the apple (see Figure 14). Place any healing symbol or your name in the center of the symbol. Then carve your name and what you wish to heal on the black candle with the knife and place it inside the apple.

Light the candle, saying:

Goddess of the apple tree,
Purge this darkness from me.
Turn the tide and bring the dawn.
Heal my soul in Avalon.

When you are done, bury the apple outside.

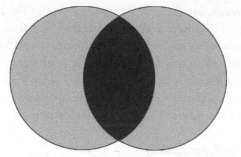

Figure 14. The vesica piscis, a shape associated with
modern-day Avalon and the Divine Feminine.

Exercise: Modron Dreaming Well

Today, devotees of Modron travel to her sacred spring in Cornwall in hopes
of gaining a prophetic message from the goddess. Tradition has it that rest-
ing or sleeping by this well induces a trance-like state in which petitioners
can commune with the goddess. And, in fact, this particular spring contains
high levels of radon, which can actually make you feel quite sleepy.

Because not everyone can travel to Cornwall to connect with Modron, I
give you this ritual to help you connect with her during your dream time. It
draws on imagery from her well, as well as on plant spirits and the magic of
water to aid you in your quest.

In this exercise, you will create a small dreaming well near your bed. To
do this, you will need:

- A small ceramic dish
- A small ceramic bowl
- Spring water
- A small handful of dirt or sand
- Mugwort
- Lavender
- Mint
- A small pouch
- A quartz sphere or tumbled stone
- An amethyst crystal
- A strip of white cotton, silk, or other natural material

Place the mugwort, lavender, and mint in the small pouch and seal it with
three knots. Crush the pouch between your hands and place it in a comfortable place on or near your pillow where you can smell it. You may also want

Celtic Goddess Grimoire

to brew a little tea from the same ingredients before bed. Be sure to omit the mugwort if you are pregnant or nursing.

Place the small ceramic dish on a flat surface near your bed, oriented with where your head would rest—ideally on your nightstand, but a windowsill will do. Put the small handful of sand or dirt into the dish and place the bowl on top of it. Then place the quartz sphere and amethyst inside the bowl. Pour the spring water into the bowl and use the incantation below to charm the water.

Mother Modron, grant me your sight.
Lend me your wisdom while I dream tonight.

Alternatively, you could say Morgan le Fae, Morgan, or Morganna.

Dip the strip of fabric into the water. You don't need to soak it, but be sure it is a little damp. Then tie this around your left wrist. Refresh the water to be sure that the bowl is full before you go to bed. In the morning, as soon as you wake up, write down any dreams you may have had in your dream journal. Then carry the water outside to a tree or bush. Place the dish on the ground, dip the fabric strip into the water again, and tie it to the tree. Gift the rest of the water to the roots of the tree.

CHAPTER 22

The Nine Maidens

Name variations: Nine Sisters, Nine Priestesses
Region: England, Wales, Cornwall, Scotland, Ireland, and more
Sacred associations: magic, healing, shapeshifting, rebirth, cauldron,
    fire, pearls, dragons, water, wells
Offerings: apples, roses, shells, sea water, lake water, hawthorn,
    spring water, candles, dragon effigies, pearls
Bodies of water: the sea, sacred springs in Glastonbury/Avalon,
    Nine Maiden's Well in Pitempton, Cauldron of Rebirth

There are many references to groups of nine maidens throughout the mythology, archaeology, and folklore of the Celtic world, including Brighid, The Cailleach, the Muses, the Korrigans, the priestesses of the Isle of Sena, the Nine Mill Maidens, the nine daughters of Ran in Norse mythology—and, of course, the Nine Sisters of Avalon with whom Morgan le Fae is connected. In fact, Morgan le Fae is mentioned in one of the earliest texts as being the chief of the nine sisters known as the Nine Sisters of Avalon.

It is important to note that these groups of nine maidens are ancient. The earliest references to these groupings of divine women go back as far as ancient cave paintings, like the Magdalenian cave paintings found in Catalonia, which could be as much as 17,000 years old. This, of course, makes it difficult to be sure of the true origins of any of these tales. Take, for instance, the Scottish tale of the nine maidens of Pitempton, who were said to have been devoured by a dragon near a sacred well. This story suggests an interesting connection to other goddesses and divine magical figures who were connected with sacred wells and could shapeshift, like Melusine. On the other hand, because the original story has been obscured by time, it is possible that these nine maidens were shapeshifting dragon goddesses rather than maidens who were devoured by the dragon.

The Nine Maidens of Annwn are vaguely mentioned in the early medieval Welsh text *Preiddeu Annwfn*, or the Spoils of Annwfn. They were said to kindle the Cauldron of Rebirth, a magical cauldron with the power to resurrect the dead. They do this with their breath, which creates another interesting link to dragons, who also breathe fire. Moreover, as we saw in chapter 21, Annwn and Avalon are both connected to the Celtic Otherworld and may be derivitave of each other.

The Nine Maidens of Annwn are also connected to the spirit realms, as they reside in the Celtic Otherworld. The number nine may also connect them with the sisters and priestesses of Avalon. The image of the cauldron further deepens this connection, because it is a vessel closely associated with water, a link made stronger by the fact that the cauldron is described as being rimmed with pearls, which are associated with water and the sea. They are also a symbolic representation of rebirth because of how they are formed— from a grain of sand that begins as an irritant—something unwanted— that is transformed into a pearl through the protective reaction of the oyster.

The Nine Maidens of Annwn are sometimes thought of as priestesses, sometimes as faery women, and sometimes as Otherworldly specters, although the latter two are probably diminished titles. It is more likely, in fact, that these maidens may have been more than priestesses, faeries, or sorceresses, and may very well have been goddesses in their own right. They seem to be consistently connected to water or vessels, and there are a number of wells dedicated to them across the Celtic world. It is also interesting that groups of nine maidens appear in Icelandic and Nordic mythology, where they are also associated with water.

Exercise: Avalonian Simmer Pot

This exercise is a great way to connect with either Morgan le Fae or the Nine Maidens of Annwn. To perform it, you will need:

- A cauldron that has a heat source or a pot on your stove
- Spring water
- 9 pinches of peppermint
- 9 hawthorn berries
- 9 rose hips
- 9 pinches of lavender
- 9 dried rose buds or 9 large pinches of fresh rose petals
- 9 small pinches of mugwort
- 9 large pinches of rosemary
- 3 slices of dried apples, cut so that the pentagram shows

Place the cauldron on its heat source (or the pot on the stove) and fill it three-quarters full with spring water. As you bring the water to a simmer, use your finger to draw a pentagram over the top of the vessel, saying:

Beautiful Sister of Nine,
Bless my simmer pot with your magic divine!

Then begin adding your ingredients.

To dry your own apples, preheat your oven to about 200° F. Place apple slices (cut so that the pentagram shows) on a small rack and put the rack on a cookie sheet. Bake them for several hours until they are dry. They will keep for several weeks this way and can be added to other magical workings and charms.

Exercise: Kindling the Cauldron of Rebirth

This is a ritual you can use to reach out to the Nine Maidens to help you kindle the Cauldron of Rebirth when you need to renew yourself or move forward on your path. If you have just come through a dark place in your life and are ready to write a new chapter, or even to begin all over again, use this ritual to help you focus on what needs to change in your life, letting the old life fade away. Then allow yourself to feel the freedom of starting over.

For this exercise, you will need:

- A small cauldron, preferably ceramic or brass
- Pearls
- 9 white candles
- Spring water collected on the dark of the moon
- Paper and pencil or pen
- A lighter
- A towel
- White rose petals

Prepare the cauldron by attaching the pearls around the rim, either by gluing them permanently in place or by wrapping a strand around the top. Be creative here and do what you feel is best. Place the nine candles around the cauldron. I recommend using tea lights, but this is your ritual, so do what feels right to you.

On the dark of the moon, travel to a sacred well and gather spring water in a vessel that you can carry back to your home altar. If you don't have access to a sacred well, try using river water. This is best done in the dark, so bring a light source with you so you can stay safe. Be sure to gather the water in silence while contemplating what was and what is about to be. Bring the water back to your home altar.

Set your space by placing a towel on the floor to catch any water that may flow off your body. On the paper, write down all the things in your life that you want to purge. Are you moving forward from a divorce? Write your ex-partner name and some of your feelings about that on the paper—especially those that you are having the most difficulty removing from your mind and spirit. As you do this, gently acknowledge your feelings. Sometimes rocking back and forth a little or inducing a light trance state can help you process everything you have gone through.

As you move through this ritual, allow yourself time to move through the pain, but be gentle with yourself. You have been through the darkness of the underworld, and this can be incredibly hard to do. If you cry, allow your tears to fall into the cauldron if you can. When you feel ready to move forward, light the nine candles one by one. Gaze at them and see the room go from darkness to light. See how the flame of each candle dances and kindles the cauldron in the center. When you are ready to let go of the old and invite in the new, light the paper with the candles and quickly place it in the cauldron. Let it burn completely to ash. If any of the paper remains unburned, use a small pair of tongs to pick it up and light it again.

Once the paper is completely turned to ash in the center of the cauldron, pick up the vessel containing the water and hold it between your hands. Begin to visualize what is to come. Visualize your favorite version of you—who you are and what you are to become. Be sure to allow for your full potential to come through. As you do this, take a deep breath, place your mouth near the surface of the water, and speak this visualization into existence. Make sure that the water is disturbed and that you can see physical movement on its surface. When you are done speaking, take another deep breath and repeat the process. Do this a total of nine times. It may help to write a sentence or two to help you remember.

When you are finished, pour a little of the water into the cauldron and use your finger to mix it with the ash. Then anoint your third eye, your eyelids, your lips, your heart center, and your hands and feet with the ash mixture on your finger. Pour the rest of the water over your head, allowing the waters of rebirth to flow from the vessel and onto your body. Sit back and visualize yourself emerging from the cauldron, whole and ready for a new perspective on life.

Finally, take a large handful of white rose petals and sprinkle them on top of your altar and cauldron. Do take care if your candles are still lit not to set anything on fire! Take another large handful of rose petals and sprinkle them over your head, your arms and legs, and the rest of your body. Sit in silence for a few moments, then open your eyes feeling refreshed and ready to begin anew! Gather the rest of the rose petals and dry them. You can use them in future rituals to help you move forward and to remind you not to slip back into old habits.

Figure 15. Glastonbury Tor, a location often described as a faery mound, similar to the Mound of Arberth.

PART VI

Goddesses of Magic

CHAPTER 23

Arianrhod—Woman of Power

Name variations: Aranrot, Aranrhod
Region: Llandwrog in northwest Wales; Dina Dinlleu on the coast
   of Caernarfonshire, Wales
Sacred associations: weaving, time, fate, silver wheel, revolving cas-
   tle, Corona Borealis, fertility, moon
Offerings: truth, silver coins, woven goods
Body of water: seacoast of Caernarfonshire, Wales

Arianrhod, whose name means "silver wheel," is a Welsh goddess whom
many consider to be a faery woman. Her story, which comes from the fourth
branch of *The Mabinogi*, is one of sadness, anger, and betrayal, but it is also
a story about sovereignty, boundaries, and standing up to bad behavior
against you.

In *The Mabinogi*, Arianrhod is identified as the daughter of Dôn, but
in other texts she is given as the daughter of Beli, son of the Druid king
Mynogan. She is connected to the moon, as well as to movement, time, and
spinning. There is also a celestial connection beyond that of the meaning of
her name and its correlation with the moon. Her castle, located in Wales not
far from Dina Dinlleu on the coast of Caernarfonshire, was called Caer Sidi
or Caer Arianrhod. This was described as a revolving castle, reflecting her
connection to time and movement. Its name is the same as the name for the
Corona Borealis, also known as the Northern Crown.

Arianrhod is known to many as the virgin mother, but I see her as the
mother of fate. Like many other Celtic goddesses, the only record of her
that survives dates from the Christian era, when she was portrayed as a

villain—a cold-hearted mother who denied her child what was rightfully his. Although Christian writers tried to diminish her from goddess to angry villain, key portions of her story indicate that she is of magical and Other-worldly origin, having survived male oppression and masculine control over her body. Her story goes like this.

A Welsh king named Math could only rule if his feet rested in the lap of a virgin during times of peace. Gwydion, son of Dôn, advised him to send for his sister, Arianrhod, who was Math's niece. When she entered court, he asked her if she was a virgin, to which she replied "yes." To determine if she was telling the truth, Math bent a magical wand and placed it on the floor, telling her to step over it. As she did so, Arianrhod gave birth to a strong golden-haired boy, causing her to panic and run for the door. As she ran, a small blob dropped onto the floor. Gwydion grabbed it before anyone could see, wrapped it in silk, and placed it in a small chest at the foot of his bed.

Math adopted the golden-haired boy and baptized him Dylan. As soon as the boy was baptized, however, he ran toward the sea and jumped into the water, instantly transforming into a sea creature.

About a year later, as Gwydion was sleeping in his bed chamber, he heard faint crying coming from the chest at the foot of his bed. When he opened the chest, he found a tiny boy waving his arms, having freed himself from the folds of silk. Gwydion brought the boy to a wet nurse, who fed him for a year. At the end of that year, he was a sturdy two-year-old and grown enough to go to court.

Some time later, as Gwydion and the boy were walking toward Caer Arianrhod, they were greeted by Arianrhod herself, who inquired who the boy was. When Gwydion replied that he was her son, she was outraged that Gwydion had hidden the child from her for so long and asked what his name was. When Gwydion said that he was nameless, Arianrhod decreed that the child would have no name unless it was given by her. At this, Gwydion began hurling insults at her, calling her a wicked woman and attacking her for no longer being a virgin.

The next day, Gwydion decided to deceive Arianrhod by conjuring up a boat and sailing to Caer Arianrhod, where he and the little boy disguised themselves as cobblers. When Arianrhod sent for the cobblers to make her some shoes, Gwydion wickedly fooled her by first making her shoes too big, and then making them too small. Eventually, he got her to come to the boat, where she greeted him with blessings of prosperity. Just then, a small wren landed on the deck of the ship and the little boy aimed at it and hit it in the leg. Arianrhod laughed and said: "The fair-haired one (Lleu Llaw Gyffes) has finished with a skillful hand." Gwydion had tricked her into naming the boy. When Arianrhod realized this, she decreed a second fate—that Lleu Llaw Gyffes would never have a weapon until she gave it to him. Gwydion responded with more verbal abuse.

Some time later, when Lleu Llaw Gyffes had grown into a young man, Gwydion decided that he needed his own weapons and determined to deceive Arianrhod yet again. Together, he and the boy set out toward Caer Arianrhod. As they approached the castle gate, they once again disguised themselves—this time as poets. Gwydion called upon his magical powers to make Arianrhod think that the harbor had been invaded. So Arianrhod gathered together weapons and armor. Gwydion armed himself, while Arianrhod armed Lleu Llaw Gyffes. Gwydion had once again tricked her, this time into arming the young boy. In response, Arianrhod decreed a third fate—that Lleu Llaw Gyffes would never have a human wife. And here ends the story of Arianrhod, which continues with the story of Blodeuwedd in the next chapter.

Exercise: Creating Silver-Wheel Moon Water

An old Scottish method for making charmed water is to add a piece of silver to it and stir it while speaking a prayer or incantation. Today, moon water is very popular and used by many witches and Pagans. Here, I combine these two watery practices and add some sacred associations to Arianrhod to create silver-wheel moon water.

For this exercise, you will need a black bowl and some spring or ocean water. Depending on your intent, you may want to select spring water, which is good for just about every use. If you want to connect with the energies of the sea, where Caer Arianrhod stands, consider using sea water. You will also need a silver coin or a silver pendant—one that is round and moonlike or has a wheel on it.

On the night of a Full Moon, take the bowl, water, and coin outside. Find a place where the light of the moon shines down on the bowl. For best results, place it so you can see a reflection of the moon or any light of the moon on the water. You may have to tip the bowl and hold it while you speak the incantation below in order to capture the moonlight.

Place the silver coin in the bowl, capture the moonlight on the surface of the water, and say:

> Lady of the silver moon,
> I enchant this water with sacred tune.
> Silver light, shine down from above.
> Bless this water with luck and love.

Stir the water with your finger nine times in a clockwise direction—moving the water around in the same way that Caer Arianrhod revolves. Then speak this prayer to Arianrhod:

> Lady of the Wheel of Fate,
> For you this Full Moon I patiently wait.
> I honor your celestial divinity,
> Show me my power through femininity.
> Stand strong with me when I'm about to say no
> And urge me on when I am too scared to go.
> Weave a magical fate for me and mine,
> Through my life, time after time.
> Arianrhod, you of the silver wheel,
> At your altar I patiently kneel.
> Gracious goddess, weave your will through me
> So I rise in balance like the tides of the sea.
> Lady of the Web of Fate,
> To you my heart, it gravitates.

CHAPTER 24

Blodeuwedd—Sovereign One

Name variations: Blodeuedd, Flowerface
Region: Wales
Sacred associations: flowers, owl, sovereignty, broom, meadowsweet,
    oak
Offerings: flowers, feathers
Body of water: River Cynfael

The story of Blodeuwedd begins where the story of Arianrhod left off. Because Arianrhod denied Lleu Llaw Gyffes a human wife, Math and Gwydion conspired to create a wife for him. They combined the flowers of oak, meadowsweet, and broom with their magic and conjured up a wife from the Otherworld, naming her Blodeuedd, which means "flowers." Blodeuedd was a beautiful Otherworldy woman who was created by men for a specific purpose—to be the perfect wife, one who would be dutiful and do all that was expected of her.

One day while Lleu Llaw Gyffes was away, Blodeuedd invited a stranger who was passing by the castle gate to dine with her. He had just been on a successful hunt and was tired, so he accepted the invitation and changed out of his riding clothes. As soon as he joined her for dinner, the two fell deeply in love and, that night, they slept together. In the morning, Blodeuedd asked him to stay another night and they feasted and made love again. Blodeuedd knew that her husband would return home soon, so, between them, they devised a plan that would allow them to stay together. Blodeuedd would pretend that she was still faithful and dutiful to her husband, all the while trying to find a way to kill him.

Noticing that his wife was sad, Lleu Llaw Gyffes asked her what was wrong. When she replied that she was worried that he would die before her, he told her that it he would not be easy to kill, because he could only be killed by a special spear—one that had been forged over the course of a year on Sundays while everyone was away at Mass. Moreover, he said, he could not be killed either indoors or out, nor on horseback or on foot. He could only be killed while on a riverbank with one foot on the back of a goat and one foot on the edge of a tub with a water-tight arched roof. Only if the special spear struck him while he was in this strange position would it bring about his death.

Blodeuedd and her lover immediately began to prepare the curious tub, forge the special spear, and set up the rest of the strange conditions. When all was ready, she invited her husband to bathe. When all the conditions were met, her lover threw the special spear, piercing Lleu Llaw Gyffes, who immediately turned into an eagle and flew away.

Blodeuedd and her lover were happy for some time, until Gwydion and Math decided to find out what had happened to Lleu Llaw Gyffes. When Blodeuedd heard they were coming, she fled to the mountains with her maidens. They crossed the River Cynfael, but were so afraid that they kept looking back. Because they were not concentrating on the path, they all fell into the river and drowned except Blodeuedd.

Gwydion eventually caught up with Blodeuedd, but decided not to kill her. Instead, he changed her into an owl because of the shame she had brought on her husband. As part of her punishment, he decreed that all other birds would be hostile toward her and would strike at her and peck her whenever they saw her. Thus she would be called Blodeuwedd, which means "owl."

Arianrhod's anger leaks into this story as the result of her rejection of her son, who then seeks Math's help to create a wife for him. Thus Blodeuedd was created from the beauty of the natural world and ultimately sought love at all costs. Her crime was that she found love where she wasn't suppose to.

Exercise: Chant for Choosing Yourself
The power of Arianrhod and Blodeuwedd lies in their ability to exert their power over the oppressive male forces in their lives—their ability to choose

themselves over masculine power. Here is a chant that you can use as an affirmation to connect to this power in yourself.

I choose myself;
I choose to be free.
I choose myself;
I choose sovereignty!
I break these chains that bind;
I tear down the façades that blind.
I crash down the cage that holds;
I reach through the magic folds.
I choose myself;
I choose to be free.
I choose sovereignty.

CHAPTER 25

Cerridwen—Sorceress and Shapeshifter

Name variations: Ceridwen, Kyrridven, Cerituen, Kerituen
Region: Gwynedd in Wales
Sacred associations: cauldron, sows and pigs, greyhounds, otters,
    hawks, herbs, rebirth, sacred rage, healing, Awen (divine inspi-
    ration), journeying through land, sea, and sky
Offerings: lake water, pearls, grain
Body of water: Lake Bala, aka Llyn Tegid

Cerridwen is a Welsh goddess and faery woman associated with inspiration, sorcery, and shapeshifting. Her name means "crooked woman," "blessed
woman," and, in some contexts, "fair and loved" or even "holy poetry."
Because of her connection to Lake Bala, she can be considered a Lake Lady,
but I have chosen to group her with goddesses of magic because of her skills
brewing Awen and her ability to shapeshift. In fact, Cerridwen's fascinating, magical, and many-layered story is replete with magic and sorcery. She
is honored by many modern practitioners and many have learned lessons
from her related to shapeshifting, the herbal arts, potion-making, and the
mysteries of death and rebirth. She is also associated with motherhood and
the wrathful woman. For the many who honor her, she is a diverse figure
with many aspects.

The meaning of this goddess's name is the subject of some debate. Its
meaning of "crooked woman" may indicate that she has a crone aspect. And,
in fact, many modern practitioners work with her as a crone goddess. It is
important to note, however, that there is no significant evidence to indicate
that she was seen as either a crone or a crone goddess. There is sufficient

evidence, however, to interpret her as a mother goddess, as her story revolves around her children and she is credited with giving birth to Taliesin. The fact that her name may also mean "blessed woman" indicates her magical aspect and her ability to brew magical potions. On the other hand, the meaning of "fair and loved" or "holy poetry" suggests her connection to Awen, or divine inspiration. All these alternative meanings seem to fit well within her story and reflect the depths and layers of her character.

Cerridwen lived in the middle of Llyn Tegid, which today is called Lake Bala, with her husband, Tegid Voel, her incredibly beautiful daughter, Creirwy, and her son, Morvran ab Tegid, also known as Avagddu. Unfortunately, Avagddu was considered quite ugly and dull, and no one believed he would go very far in life because of his lack of skills and beauty. So Cerridwen, being a good and loving mother, set out to change his fate.

Cerridwen knew that she could not change her son's looks, so she decided to brew him a potion that would bring him inspiration and scientific knowledge that would make him appear more favorably in the eyes of the nobles. She set up her cauldron, lit a fire, and began to gather herbs in alignment with astrological and planetary positions. Each day, for a year and a day, she gathered herbs and added them to the potion simmering in her cauldron, her goal being to brew three drops of Awen, the elixir of inspiration.

As she toiled over her cauldron, she realized that she needed someone to help tend it and stir the potion while she went to gather herbs. So she hired a little boy named Gwion Bach to help her and tasked an old blind man named Morda to watch over him. Each day, Gwion Bach stirred the cauldron, while Cerridwen left to gather herbs.

After a year and a day, the elixir was ready. As Gwion Bach was giving it a final stir, three small drops splashed up and landed on his finger. The potion was hot and, in his surprise, he put his finger in his mouth to cool the burn, ingesting the three drops of Awen. Cerridwen was furious that, after all her hard work, little Gwion Bach and not her son had received the Awen. She became so angry that she picked up a piece of wood and struck Morda on the head, causing his eye to fall out and hang down onto his cheek. The cauldron then broke in two and the rest of the potion became poison, flowing onto the ground and poisoning the land.

Celtic Goddess Grimoire

Because he had ingested the three drops of Awen, Gwion Bach received the gift of second sight and could see everything in the past and everything yet to come. Knowing he had to protect himself from Cerridwen's fierce anger, he ran, pursued by the goddess. When he became tired, he shapeshifted into a hare so he could outrun her. But Cerridwen turned herself into a fast greyhound and followed. When she caught up to Gwion in his hare form, he headed for the river and flung himself in, turning himself into a fish. Cerridwen shapeshifted into an otter and continued her pursuit, chasing him through the water. When she caught up to him again, he transformed into a small songbird and took to the sky. Cerridwen shapeshifted once again, this time into a hawk that chased Gwion through the sky until he became tired. Seeing a heap of grain below, he flew down and, when he was near it, turned himself into a single piece of grain thinking he would be lost in the pile. But Cerridwen turned into a hen and devoured all the grain—and Gwion Bach along with it.

Gwion remained in Cerridwen's belly for nine months, until she gave birth to a beautiful male child. When she saw how beautiful he was, she found she could not kill him, so she bound him in a leather bag and tossed him into the sea. There, he was found by Gwyddno and his son Elphin. When Gwyddno saw how beautiful the boy was, he said "behold the radiant brow" and named him Taliesin.

As you think about Cerridwen's story, ask yourself what it means to you. What can you learn from it? What can the characters in it teach you and what can you learn about your own life from the pursuit of Gwion Bach? What are you chasing in your own life? When Cerridwen comes into your life, she may show up as an initiator who is there to facilitate change, or as a loving mother who is there to protect and defend. She may teach you to have patience and understanding when a long-term project goes awry. Or she may teach you to overturn your cauldron and chase after what is rightfully yours. She may teach you the knowledge of herbs and potions, or the mysteries and power of the cauldron. Whatever lesson you learn will be sure to enhance your life and help you along your path.

Exercise: Invocation to Cerridwen

Use this invocation to connect with Cerridwen and call down the blessings of her lessons.

Mother of Transformation,
I call upon your name.
Cauldron-keeper,
Potion-brewer,
Great mother of the lake.
Cerrid-wen,
Cerrid-wen,
Cerr–id–wen.

Exercise: Shapeshifting with Cerridwen

Much of Cerridwen's story centers around her ability to shapeshift. To shapeshift with Cerridwen, you will need a cauldron—either copper or brass—or a cast-iron pot. You will also need a rectangular piece of paper, a pen or pencil, and a lighter.

Turn your piece of paper onto its horizontal axis, then draw a line down the center, creating two sections. Take a few deep breaths and contemplate the things you love about yourself and the things that need to change or be removed, or qualities and characteristics into which you may want to shapeshift.

Once you have this in your mind, sketch or write out things that represent the qualities you love about yourself on one side of the line you have drawn. Be sure to focus on where you have come from, and where you are right now. You can use words to describe yourself or draw a picture of yourself as you are right now.

Take a few deep breaths and focus on what you want to become. What changes do you want to make? What qualities and experiences do you want to bring into your life? How do you want to transform yourself? When you have these firmly in your mind, tear the paper in half, keeping the blank half in front of you. Place the half on which you have written into the cauldron and light it using the lighter. Watch it as it burns.

When it is completely burned to ash, dip your finger into the ash and use it to draw the Awen symbol on the blank half of the paper in front of you (see Figure 16). It may not show up perfectly, but that is okay as long as the symbol appears in ash on the paper.

Write or sketch what you want to shift into on the paper—again you can use either words or images—then fold the paper into a small square.

Figure 16. Awen symbol. Draw this on the blank half of your paper with your finger.

Gather up the ash in your cauldron and take it and the folded paper outside to a place where you can dig a small hole. When the hole is ready, sprinkle some ash in the bottom of it, add the folded paper, then add the rest of the ashes. Cover everything with dirt and speak this invocation, or words of your own choosing:

> As Cerridwen once brewed her potion of Awen,
> So now does the Awen flow through me.
> As Cerridwen once carried the Divine Child,
> So now does the earth.
> As Cerridwen shifted her shape with ease,
> So now do I shift my shape.

Be sure to travel back to Cerridwen's shrine to give thanks and offerings, or to seek her wisdom.

Exercise: Cauldron of Inspiration Simmer Pot

For this exercise, you will need a cauldron that can be heated from the bottom. A stove-top sauce pan can work as well. Place it on the stovetop and fill it with water. As you heat the water to a simmer, add the herbs below:

- Cedar (sun)
- Rose (Venus)
- Lavender (Mercury)
- Mugwort (earth)
- Mullein (Saturn)
- Juniper (Jupiter)
- Hawthorn (Mars)
- Vervain (Sirius)
- White rose (moon)

Exercise: Inspiration Tea

Brew yourself an herbal tea to bring you inspiration using the following herbs:

- 1 tbs rose petals
- Small pinch of mugwort (skip if pregnant or nursing)
- Small pinch of vervain

- 1 tbs lavender
- 1 tbs chamomile
- 1 tbs hawthorn flowers

Place the herbs in a mason jar and fill with boiling water. Allow them to steep for several minutes. You may want to let them settle to the bottom before drinking. When you are ready to drink the tea, use a mesh wire strainer to strain the infused tea into a cup and enjoy!

PART VII

Horse Goddesses

CHAPTER 26

Rhiannon—The Great Queen

Name variations: Rigantona
Region: Wales, Gorsedd Arberth near Castle Narberth
Sacred associations: veils, horses, magical birds, magical bags,
    bowls, collars, donkeys, liminality, the Otherworld, white
    animals, sovereignty
Offerings: feathers, effigies of horses, honey, flowers
Body of water: the ocean, where her birds are

Rhiannon is a Welsh goddess whose name means "Great Queen." Her story, which appears in *The Mabinogi*, is one of love, betrayal, faith, and sovereignty. Rhiannon was the daughter of Hyfaidd Hen and the mother of Pryderi. She was the wife of Pwyll, Prince of Dyfed, and later, after his passing, became the wife of Manawydan, brother of Brân the Blessed. Her complicated story goes like this.

Prince Pwyll set off on a hunt with his entourage and soon came upon a beautiful young maiden with a veiled face riding a white horse. He was so taken by her beauty that he decided to give up the hunt and pursue her. Although he rode for hours, he was never able to catch up to her. Finally, in frustration, he called out, asking her to stop. She laughed and, pulling back her veil, told him that all he had to do was ask and she would have stopped. She then told him that she had been promised in marriage to a man named Gwawl, but that she would prefer to marry him. So they decided to wed.

A year passed and soon it was time for their wedding feast. It was here that Pwyll was approached by Gwawl, who asked him for a favor. Pwyll, not knowing that Gwawl was Rhiannon's former bethrothed, gladly agreed, saying he would give Gwawl anything he wanted. Gwawl demanded

Rhiannon's hand in marriage. Rhiannon told Pwyll that, having given his word, he must comply or be disgraced. But she assured him that, although she might be forced to marry Gwawl, he would never have her. When Pwyll asked how this would come to pass, she gave him a little bag and told him to keep it with him always. She then asked for a year to prepare for her wedding to Gwawl and gave Pwyll strict instructions that, in one year, he was to come to her wearing rags and carrying the bag, leaving ninety-nine horsemen hidden in the orchard near the castle.

When the year had passed and Rhiannon and Gwawl's wedding feast was underway, Pwyll entered wearing rags and carrying the bag, which he asked to be filled with food. Although a great deal of food was put into the bag, it never seemed to be full. Through a series of deceptions, Pwyll forced Gwawl to renounce his betrothal to Rhiannon, and she and Pwyll were married.

Rhiannon and Pwyll were very happy in their marriage and Rhiannon eventually gave birth to a beautiful baby boy named Pryderi. Exhausted by the birth, Rhiannon fell asleep, asking her nursemaids to care for the child. But they fell asleep as well and, in the morning, the baby was nowhere to be found. Knowing they would be held responsible for the loss of the child, they panicked and conspired to hide his disappearance. So they killed a small dog and smeared its blood on Rhiannon and scattered the bones around. When she awoke, the nursemaids told her that she had eaten her baby, claiming that the smeared blood and scattered bones were all that remained of the child.

When he was told this, Pwyll, fearing it was true, began to suspect Rhiannon. As the dreadful tale spread, the nobles pressured him to divorce his wife for her evil deeds. But Pwyll began to have doubts and refused to do so. The pressure from the nobles became so great, however, that he was left with no other choice but to punish her. He decreed that she must stand outside the castle walls near the mounting block for seven years and carry the load of every traveler who came to the castle, as if she were a horse. Rhiannon suffered her punishment for years without complaint.

Not long after the terrible night Pryderi was stolen, on May Eve, Teyrnon Twrf Laint, lord of Gwent Is Coed, was tending to one of his mares that was about to give birth. The foal was born and it was perfect in every way. But then Teyrnon Twrf Laint heard a strange noise and saw a large claw reach through the window and snatch up the foal. He flung open the door and chased after the beast. Then he remembered that he had left the door open in his haste and returned home. When he arrived there, he found a small boy wrapped in silk swaddling lying in the barn. He and his wife had never been able to conceive, so, since they didn't know where the child had come from, they decided to care for him as their own and named him Gwri Wallt Euryn. The boy, who had beautiful golden hair, thrived and grew strong.

When, after years had passed, the couple eventually heard of Rhiannon's struggles, they knew deep down that the boy they had raised was hers. So they decided they had no choice but to return him to his parents and free Rhiannon from her punishment. When they arrived at the front gate of the castle, Rhiannon met them and asked to carry their load. They explained who the boy was, and the likeness between Pwyll and Pryderi was so strong that no one at court doubted that this was his son. Rhiannon was cleared of all charges and lived with Pwyll in happiness for many years.

After some time, Pwyll passed from this world into the ancestral realms. Pryderi, now grown, realized that his mother was sad and lonely, so he took it upon himself to find her a companion and introduced her to his friend Manawydan. They soon wed, and Rhiannon embarked on yet another adventure.

While out riding one day with Manawydan, Pryderi entered a mysterious fort that had appeared overnight. In the middle of the fort was a beautiful golden bowl with chains reaching up to the heavens. Enchanted by the bowl, he touched it and froze in place. When Manawydan returned to tell Rhiannon what had happened to her son, she set out to find this magical place. When she did, she entered the fort, touched the bowl, and also froze in place. That night, the fort disappeared—along with Rhiannon and Pryderi. After this, a series of enchantments cursed the land. Many people were turned into mice and Rhiannon was turned into a mule. But Manawydan was able to negotiate the release of Rhiannon and Pryderi from these enchantments, and they were returned to their human form.

Rhiannon appears once again in *The Mabinogi* in the story of Culhwch and Olwen, which contains a single mention of Adar Rhiannon, or "the birds of Rhiannon." These magical birds are said to live far away in the ocean and have the ability to wake the dead and lull the living to sleep. They are never seen, but they are said to have the ability to sing and be heard from far away, while sounding as if they were present.

Rhiannon's tale is rich in many-layered symbolism. For instance, her veil may be symbolic of a veil between the realms and indicate that she is a liminal spirit. It may be significant that, when Pwyll first sees Rhiannon, he sees her through a veil, as if in a vision or with prophetic sight. Did he see her through the veil because she was in the faery realms? Was she indeed in this world, or was he peering through the veil and observing her in the Otherworld? Was he seeing a vision of her? No matter which explanation you choose, there is certainly an Otherworldy element at play here.

Rhiannon's white horse may be another indication of her Otherworldly and liminal nature, since white animals, especially those with red eyes or red-tipped ears, were thought to be from the Otherworld. White, red, and black animals are seen as magical in the Celtic world and are used in many symbolic ways. Many Celtic-based Pagan groups use them as well. The speed with which Rhiannon rides is also interesting, and may be considered as part of her magical and liminal nature. Folklore tells us that, in the realms of the faery folk, time passes differently than it does in the physical realm, which may account for Pwyll's difficulty catching her. Perhaps the reason he could never catch up to her is that she was never really in the physical plane at all—at least not until he asked her to stop. When he does, she chooses to move from the liminal to the physical realm, reenforcing her association with sovereignty.

In fact, three horses play a role in Rhiannon's story, a number that has ties to magic and to esoteric mysteries. The first is the white horse she rides when Pwyll chases her—perhaps a liminal horse that can travel from the faery realm to the physical realm. The second appears when she becomes like a horse as part of her punishment. The third appears when she is changed into a mule, an animal closely analogous to a horse. While the first horse was a beautiful, majestic beast, the other two are workhorses, beasts of burden.

Birds appear in parts of Rhiannon's tale as well, again supporting her magical nature and linking her to other magical bird-like women like the Greek sirens, Blodeuwedd, and even Morgan le Fae, who is sometimes described as having wings and shapeshifting abilities. And her magical bag may also be significant, as magical garments like the golden fleece and magical bags appear in many Greek myths. The enchantments that curse the land

and finally turn Rhiannon into a mule may be symbolic of lost sovereignty, forcing her to act against her will.

Sovereignty, forgiveness, and patience seem to be the key lessons of Rhiannon's tale. Her patience in waiting for Pwyll to ask her to stop the chase on horseback, her understanding when he promised Gwawl more than he should have, and her forgiveness of him for condemning her to a cruel punishment all speak to Rhiannon's power of choice and her sovereignty. Abandonment, betrayal, and loneliness play a large part in her story as well.

There are several locations associated with Rhiannon. Among them are Dyfed, a very large tract of land that encompassed most of western Wales; Presli, which has been identified as the place where the stones that make up Stonehenge were quarried; and the Mound of Arberth, which is described as a place of prophecy and may have represented a balancing point in the Celtic Otherworld that is resonant of the *axis mundi*. This location may have been seen as a faery mound within which faery folk resided, similar to Glastonbury Tor (see Figure 15). Annwn, or Annwfn, is also mentioned, although this is less about physical landscape and more about the Celtic Otherworld.

Although Rhiannon's story is one of suffering, it is also one that teaches us to have faith and trust in ourselves, to value patience and persistence, and to retain our sovereignty. While this tale is quite old, reverence for and worship of the Great Queen is still alive in the hearts of many Celtists, witches, Pagans, Druids, and other magical folk. The song *Rhiannon* by Stevie Nicks has become a modern anthem for many witches and is used by some practitioners to get into a magical mood, to call upon Rhiannon, or to sing as a devotional offering. Many look to Nicks for witchy lifestyle tips and her nickname as the Gossamer Witch has earned her status in the modern mind as a pillar of the mystical and magical communities.

Exercise: Invocation to Rhiannon
Use this invocation to call on the power of Rhiannon when you need to reassert your sovereignty or feel forced to act against your will.

Rhiannon, Great Queen,
Come forth from the faery mound unseen.
Rhiannon, I call to you;
Show me strength that is true.

Come to me swiftly like your white horse.
When life derails me, be my strength and recourse.
Veiled Otherworldy woman of beauty,
Show me how to show up to my sacred duty.
Beautiful faery woman, when life is skewed,
Comfort me and lend me your strength and fortitude.

Exercise: Charm Bag to Heal Wounds of Betrayal

As we have seen, charm bags were often used for protection and healing. Here's one you can use to heal wounds of betrayal.

For this exercise you will need:

- A small red bag or square of cloth
- A white string or ribbon
- A white cloth
- Pen or pencil

- A cauldron or a metal bowl in which you can burn something
- A handful of seeds from a plant or flower that grows easily in your region
- 3 feathers

Be sure to start this ritual on the dark of the moon.

Sit quietly somewhere and write down your feelings and thoughts about times you have felt betrayed, along with the names and actions of those who have betrayed you. Pour your heart out here and allow yourself to really feel the emotions as you do. When you are finished, crumple up the paper and place it in the red bag. Wrap the white string around the bag three times and tie it in a bow.

Place the bag on your altar and cover it with the white cloth. As you do, visualize sending it into the Otherworld to be held and cared for by Rhiannon. Leave the bag on your altar for as long as you need. Whenever feelings from this betrayal creep into your mind and heart, sit down and write it all out on another piece of paper. Crumple that paper, remove the white cloth from over the bag, untie the bag, and place the paper inside. Then retie the bag and cover it again with the white cloth. Do this for as long as you need to, even if that is over several weeks or months.

When you feel you are ready to complete the process, uncover your charm bag and empty all the crumpled paper into the cauldron. Add the three feathers and light it all on fire. Allow the paper and feathers to burn down until all that is left is ash. As you do, contemplate Rhiannon's magical birds and how they have the power to sing the living to sleep and the dead awake. Contemplate this transformation and how you can take things like pain in your own life and watch them die. Ask Rhiannon to bring new life and happiness to the spaces in your heart where there was once pain.

When you are ready, mix the handful of seeds with the ash and put them in the bag. Wrap it with the white string again and place it on your altar. This time, as you cover the bag with the white cloth, ask Rhiannon to transform your pain into something beautiful and magnificent. On the next Full Moon, unveil the bag, plant the seeds in your garden or a pot of soil, or scatter them in a field where you can watch them grow. Water the seeds to help them flourish. When the plants bloom, pick the flowers and give them as offerings to Rhiannon as thanks for helping transform your pain into something beautiful and new.

CHAPTER 27

Epona—The Great Mare

Name variations: Eponina, Epotia
Region: Gaul, Great Britian
Sacred associations: horses, fertility, baskets of fruit, patera, keys,
    serpents, wheat, cornucopia, prosperity, earth's bounty
Offerings: grain, horse effigies, coins, offering bowls full of fruit
Body of water: River Rhine

Epona is a horse goddess who was worshiped across a wide range of regions from England to the Alps. She was most popular in continental Europe and her cult is believed to have originated in the Rhineland with the Germanic tribes. She was worshiped widely throughout the Roman Empire, where she was petitioned by Roman soldiers who venerated her in return for protection of themselves and their horses in battle. Epona's name is Gaulish in origin and translates as "The Great Mare." There are no inscriptions to her in the Gaulish language, however, and most inscriptions to her that have been found are in Latin.

Epona's imagery suggests that she is of Celtic origin, but no worship of her has been documented after the Roman period. Her worship originated in Aedui and Lingones in Burgandy, areas known for raising healthy and fertile horses. Because of her associations with horses, and thus with battle, her worship in Great Britian may well have had a direct influence on the Roman occupation.

Although there is evidence of temples dedicated to Epona, shrines to her were most often placed in stables and with horses, emphasizing her role as a protectress of cavalry. In fact, the Roman poets Juvenal, Minucius Felux, and Apuleius refer to her as the "Mare-headed Mother." She is known as the patroness of horses and associated with their training, their care, and their breeding, and as guardian of the stables. Agesilaus, a Greek writer, even reports that she was born of a man and a mare.

Epona is generally depicted in three ways—riding sidesaddle on a horse carrying fruit in a patera or cornucopia, indicating her role as a fertility goddess; in what is called an "imperial pose," sitting on a central throne with a horse flanking her on either side; and on a chariot or cart drawn by horses or mules.

Horses were not only important to soldiers, however. They were also highly valued in rural areas where women focused on farming and horses were part of their work. Horses were considered to be "fruitful" and full of fertility. Epona Day was traditionally celebrated on December 18. Her feast day was celebrated on June 13.

Exercise: Invocation to Epona
Use this invocation to reach out to Epona for strength and fertility.

> Epona, swift as the mare,
> I call upon you with this prayer.
> Powerful mare-headed mother,
> You who are like no other,
> Great Mare who is strong and fast,
> Grant me your fortitude and how to outlast.
> Fruitful goddess of fertility,
> Bless me with your powers of agility!

Exercise: Horsebrass Charm for Luck
Horsebrasses are large brass medallions that are usually circular in shape, although ovals, shields, crosses, horseshoes, and hearts were sometimes used. They were placed on bridles as decorations, usually on parade horses. This tradition continued well into the 1900s, until the introduction of automobiles and mechanized farm equipment diminished the use and importance of horses. Today, they often grace the walls of pubs and are sometimes used by folk magicians, cunning folk, and witches as magical charms for luck, protection, and abundance, and to ward off the evil eye. They can be found all over the United Kingdom and in other parts of the world as well.

Horsebrasses are appropriate to use in rituals related to Epona, because they often resemble *phalera*, rounded disks or medals used by the Romans to decorate their horses and themselves for parades. Sometimes they also resemble Celtic sun disks. They are still used in parades today, often in the shape of a horsehoe, a horse, or both.

In this exercise, be sure to use a horsebrass that has a horse on it. These are the most common and should be easy to find. If you don't have a horsebrass or can't acquire one, you can use a brass figurine or pendant of a horse instead. Other metals can be substituted as well if necessary.

I suggest using green thread or yarn for your braid, because green corresponds with luck, prosperity, and abundance. You can use several different shades of green to give depth and color to the braid, or you can use a single shade of green. Loop several strands of thread or yarn through the top of the horsebrass, divide them into three sections, and braid them together. When you reach the top, knot the strands three times, while saying:

By knot of one this charm, begun.
By knot of two, I seal it true.
By knot of three, so mote it be.

Hold the finished charm between your palms and ask Epona to empower it with your intent. Then hang it on your wall.

Exercise: Horseshoe Charm for Protection

Horseshoes that are painted with a motif called "castles and roses" are popular English folk art, usually found in conjunction with the canal systems. They are traditionally hung in homes in England and all over the world to bring in luck or protect the home. In my own workings, I use a horseshoe that is painted blue and decorated with roses in the traditional rose and castle motif. You can create a similar charm empowered by Epona for protection, which can be particularly useful if you keep horses, but can also be used to protect the home.

To begin, select a horseshoe—ideally an antique or used shoe, because it will already have a strong imprint from a horse having worn it. In a pinch, you can buy a new horseshoe at your local feed or farm store.

Next, apply a base color, preferably a glossy acrylic or spray paint, and let it dry, then decorate it however you wish. Finally, add Epona's name in a different color to the center. You can also add protective symbols to the back of the horseshoe. In fact, you can decorate the rest of the horseshoe however you like, perhaps painting protective plants like blackberry, Saint John's wort, or hawthorn. Or you can choose other traditional symbols for protection.

Once the paint is dry, use a clear sealant to set it and protect it from chipping. Then hang the horseshoe over your front door. If you are using the charm for protection, be sure that the legs are pointing in the traditional downward orientation. If you are using the charm for luck, add luck and properity symbols, then hang it with the legs pointing up.

CHAPTER 28

Macha—Battle Goddess

Name variations: Macha Mong Rua
Region: Ulster, Ireland
Sacred associations: crows, horses, sovereignty, war, second sight
Offerings: feathers, effigies of horses, honey, flowers
Body of water: sacred wells found at Navan Fort

Macha is an Irish battle goddess who is one of the three sisters or aspects of The Morrigan. She is most often seen as a horse goddess, but is also associated with crows. Sometimes she is even called Macha the Crow. Macha's story has many similarities to those of Welsh faery women and goddesses. She, like Rhiannon, has associations with horses and carrying the burdens of men. Like Melusine and the Lady of Llyn y Fan Fach, her marriage comes with strict terms and conditions. As with many of the other goddesses we have discussed, there seem to be several variations of her and several different hints as to her true nature. Her story, from *Noinden Ulad* ("The Debility of the Ulstermen"), goes like this.

There once was a farmer named Crundchu mac Agnomain. One day, there was a knock on his door and, when he opened it, there stood Macha. He invited her in and she made herself at home. She began keeping house for him and helped him with the land; his home and farm flourished and he became wealthy. Soon, Macha became pregnant with his child.

Macha wed Crundchu mac Agnomain on the condition that he not brag about her to any man. But when he went to an assembly at Ulster, he could not resist the temptation to speak about her. When he saw how fast the king's horses raced, he knew that Macha could run even faster. So, despite her warning, he began bragging about his supernatural wife and how she could surely outrun the king's horses. Of course, this angered the king and he sent for Macha. She was brought to the assembly and told she must race the horses. Macha pointed out that she was in the late stages of pregnancy and begged not to race. But the king threatened to kill Crundchu if she did not, so she appealed to the crowd for help. All her pleas were rejected.

The king, convinced that his horses would win because of Macha's pregnancy, forced her to run the race. Of course, she ended up winning quite easily. But, before the king's horses even arrived at the finish line, she went into labor and gave birth to twins—a boy named Fall and a girl named Fial. Unfortunately she died giving birth to them and, as she did, she cursed the men of Ulster. She decreed that, from then on, every time the province was threatened, the warriors would go into a kind of pseudo-labor that would weaken them for five days and four nights. This continued for nine generations and the province of Ulster's capital city is named Emhain Macha, or Twins of Macha, in her honor.

There are other versions of Macha's story as well. One portrayed her as the wife of a figure called Nemedh, who was purported to be one of the first people to settle Ireland and led the third invasion of its lands. In this story, Macha had the gift of foresight and could see the future. Seeing the death and destruction that lay ahead, she died of heartbreak. In another version of her story, Macha is described as having red hair, Mong Rua, and is associated with battle. Alternatively, this may be the name of a historical figure who was queen of Ireland.

Exercise: Prayer to Macha

Macha teaches us lessons of strength, stamina, and sovereignty. You can call on her for speed and strength with this prayer.

> Sovereign goddess swift and fair,
> I call on you when I'm in need of repair.
> Show me the strength of your resolve;
> This pain and tension please dissolve.
> Show me how to run the course,
> And have the strength of a racehorse.
> Macha, I call you by name.
> Restoration and balance I do claim!

Celtic Goddess Grimoire

CONCLUSION

Return to the Standing Stones

Now that you have gotten to know a few of these goddesses and faery women, I recommend that you take a vision journey back to where we started—at the standing stones. This time, however, begin with a different intent—to know who it was that you saw in the water on your first journey. Allow the vision of the goddess to come forth once again. Speak to her and ask her name. Let her move you; let her speak to you. Perhaps see her name carved in the stone around the basin.

Arnemetia came to me years before I had found any real information about her; Anu came to my partner before he even knew her name. I have even had spirits connected to wells come to me with names that will never be uttered aloud or written in a book. So if you see a vision of an obscure or unknown goddess, don't worry. You just may have to work a little harder to get to know her. Allow her to guide you to the information you need. You will be surprised what you can find when she is leading the way to her own discovery. Trust in her.

Do some Internet and book research on the goddess who came to you in your vision. Try to answer questions like these:

- What region is she from?
- What information do we currently have about her?
- What information is missing?
- How can you begin deepening your connection to her through research?
- How can you begin deepening your connection to her through practice?
- What do you already have that connects you to her?

- What can you put on your altar that will connect you to her?
- What offerings are most appropriate?

If you feel that you have been called in service to a goddess or would like to dedicate your service to one, try creating a sacred space that can help you do just that.

Set a firm time boundary on your dedication and service—perhaps three, six, or nine months; perhaps mark cycles of a year and a day or thirteen moons. And remember, it is always good to set goals you can achieve. If you have never dedicated your practice to a goddess or spirit before, consider a short span of time—perhaps a three-month period. This will help you to discover if you have the time and space to achieve your goal. If you find that you have overextended yourself, you can easily step back to a more achievable goal at a later date. If you have chronic pain or mobility issues and can't always make it to your altar, don't state that you will! Reword your commitment so that it fits your needs—perhaps something like: "I will kneel at your altar every morning that my health allows."

When I first began my service to the Divine Feminine, I was so excited and starry-eyed that I made big promises to the spirits with whom I was working. I was able to fulfill most of them. But when I fell short, there were often consequences. Remember, Celtic women and the goddesses they worshiped were fierce. Many were worshiped by women in warrior tribes, women who held property and status in society and were not timid. Some, like Cerridwen and The Morrigan, are more intense than others. Some, like Sulis, have a reputation for cursing. Some display a full range of anger when they are betrayed by those they are working with to achieve magical goals. On the other hand, we have seen other goddesses who suffer misfortune with fortitude and strength. We have gotten to know young maiden goddesses who are full of life and mother goddesses who are full of fertility and nurturing.

To make matters even more confusing, modern-day folklore and practitioners often spout contradictory beliefs and suggest different paths when discussing the correct way to approach goddesses and the faery folk. So how do you know what portions of folklore, mythology, and archaeology you should accept and which ones are tainted by the bias of the writer? This is where wisdom, discernment, and divination can come to your aid. Of course, rigorous research and cultural understanding should always be key components in understanding the best way to move forward with a particular spirit. But inspiration and insight can also provide important information about these dynamic beings and help to guide you through the deeply layered symbolism that each contains.

The two most important factors in making sure that you are in alignment with a particular goddess before moving forward are integrity and intention. Are you being honest with yourself as you approach your practice? And are you clear about what you hope to gain by your connection to the goddess you feel compelled to serve?

Glossary of Celtic Goddesses and Faery Women

In addition to the goddesses and spirits discussed in the foregoing chapters, this glossary contains the names of many who are not explicitly discussed. I include them to help guide you as you expand your knowledge and develop your practice.

Abnoba: Sometimes called Mistress of the Forest. She is the namesake of the many rivers named Avon and is the ruler of the headwaters of the Danube. She is also associated with the Black Forest in Germany.

Achtland: Irish queen who married one of the Tuatha Dé Danann and became immortal by passing into the realms of the Sidh, or Shining Ones.

Adsagsona: Celtic goddess of magic and the Otherworld whose name means "weaver of spells." She was worshiped in continental Europe and known for being able to find any object that held a blessing or curse.

Adsullata: River goddess worshiped in the continental Celtic world, in what is today known as Austria. She was associated with the River Savus, or Sava, and was later worshiped in Brittany. Her name means "suck," "giving liquid," or "sucking liquid." She was a hot-spring goddess and the origins of the Celtic sun goddess Sul.

Aerfen: Welsh river goddess who is the personification of the River Dee. She is associated with warfare and sacrifice.

Aeval: Also Evell, Aoibheall, Aibell, Aebill, Aoibhell, Aoibhil, Aibhinn. A faery queen who is connected with the southwestern area of Munster near a faery mound at Killaloe in County Clare. Nearby is a well called the Well of Aeval, which flows forth from a rock named Craganeevul, or the Rock of Aeval. Also associated with Slieve Bernaugh, her name means "beautiful" or "lovely one." She was queen of two dozen banshees and was turned into a white cat by the sea fae Clídna.

Agrona: A warrior goddess from Britain who has been described as similar to The Morrigan.

Aibheaeg: Irish faery queen or goddess who is worshiped at the Well of Fire in Donegal.

Aífe: Also Aife, Aoife, Eefa, Aeife, Eva. There are several mentions of Aífe throughout various texts. In Scotland, she is considered a great warrior who trained other Irish heroes. She was sometimes seen as a sister or daughter of Scáthach. In some cases, she may actually be Scáthach, or perhaps her rival. She's also associated with the children of Lir and is seen as their stepmother. There's mention of her in the *Book of Invasions*, where she's listed as one of five wives of Partholón. She is also associated with the crane bag and was transformed into a crane or heron by her jealous rival. Her name means "radiant and beautiful" and her sacred associations include cranes, warriors, and swans.

Aige: Faery woman sometimes described as malicious. Aige was full of grace and charm, but filled with jealousy. A neighbor turned her into a wild doe and she wandered till she was killed by a hunter.

Aimend: Obscure Celtic solar goddess.

Ainge: One of the Dagda's daughters who had magical powers over nature and owned a cauldron that held waters that behaved like the ocean, ebbing and flowing like the tides.

Alauna: Celtic goddess found in continental Europe and Wales. She is the namesake of the River Alaunus in Brittany and the River Alun in Pembrokeshire.

Alba: Also Albinal, Albu, Albion. British goddess who was reported to be chief goddess of Britain.

Alend: Obscure Irish goddess associated with the ancient capital of Leinster. She was revered in Leinster on the Hill of Allen.

Allen: Personification of the hill that was said to have an invisible entrance into the Otherworld.

Almu: Obscure Irish goddess also associated with the ancient capital of Leinster and the Hill of Allen.

Ancamna: Continental Celtic mother goddess associated with healing and prosperity. She is also the consort of the Roman god Mars.

Andarta: Goddess associated with continental Europe who was worshiped by the Celtic tribe Voconces. Her name is similar to Andraste, so the two are often conflated, but she is more often seen as a wildlife goddess because her name contains "art," which links her with bear goddesses like Artio.

Annowre: Sorceress, faery woman, or witch who is conflated with Morgan le Fae. She lured King Arthur into the forest to seduce him. When he rejected her, she held him captive and forced him to battle other knights. Tristan and Nimue helped Arthur escape and eventually killed Annowre.

Anu: Another name for Danu.

Ardwinna: Also Arduinna, Arduenna, Arduanna, Ardwinna. Celtic goddess found in continental Europe. Some have associated her with the Roman Diana and the Greek Artemis. She has been depicted riding a wild boar in the forest, and forests were sacred to her. She welcomed hunters to her forests as long as they left her appropriate offerings for the animals they killed. She is the goddess of the Ardennes Forest.

Argante: British goddess and queen of Avalon and the Otherworld. Many believe she may be a variant form of Morgan le Fae or Arianrhod. King Arthur was taken to Argante to be healed when he was mortally wounded.

Artio: Celtic goddess associated with bears. Also called Deae Artio or Andarta.

Asenora: Princess of Brittany who was thrown into the sea in a barrel. She made it to Zennor in Cornwall and was later honored as Saint Senara. She may be a mermaid or a sea goddess.

Atesmerta: Continental Celtic goddess whose inscriptions have been found in Gaul.

Aveta: Healing spring goddess venerated in Trier, Germany. She was depicted nursing a child and also with baskets of fruit and dogs. She seems to be a goddess of fertility, abundance, and motherhood.

Badb: Irish goddess of war who was considered a war furie. Sometimes seen as one of the sisters who make up The Morrigan. Her name translates as "scald crow" or "hoodie crow," and she is often depicted as a screeching bird on the battlefield. She may also be associated with Cathubodua.

Banba: One of the three Irish goddesses of the Tuatha Dé Danann who met the Milesians when they first invaded. She was considered one of the three who ruled over the land. Her sacred symbols include hazel and pigs, and some link her with the Matronae or Deae Matres. Sometimes she is given the name Cesair.

Bé Chuille: Daughter of Flidais, who was the only warrior in the Tuatha Dé Danann to fight Carman, the wicked sorceress.

Bé Chuma: One of the Tuatha Dé Danann. She originated in the Otherworld, but left to marry Conn of the Hundred Battles, King of Tara.

Bébinn: Irish goddess of birth, sister to Bóand.

Bebo: Wife of the tiny faery king Iubdan. Most likely a faery queen as well. She became the mistress of King Fergus of Ulster for a year. Eventually, Iubdan gave King Fergus magical shoes in exchange for Bebo.

Becfhola: Queen from Tara who is considered a goddess by some. She represented sovereignty.

Belisama: British and continental Celtic goddess who was connected with the River Ribble in Lancaster. Her name means "shining" or "bright," which indicates a connection to Brighid or Sulis. The Romans connected her with Minerva, which suggests she may have had solar, fire, and sacred spring associations. She is associated with good fortune and abundance.

Berba: Irish goddess of the River Barrow.

Berecynthia: Obscure Celtic goddess found in continental Europe.

Berguisa: Goddess from Burgundy and consort of Ucuetis, a Gaulish deity who was venerated there.

Berrey Dhone: Manx goddess and giantess sometimes known as Brown Berry. She originated on the Isle of Man and was often described in ways similar to The Cailleach or as a hag witch.

Black Anis: A diminished form of an older goddess like Danu or The Cailleach. She is associated specifically with the Dane Hills and is the subject of much folklore related to hauntings, including luring children to a cave to eat them. She is said to take the form of a cat, a hare, or a cannibalistic nun.

Blai: Irish heroine who was turned into a deer and became pregnant with a son, Oisín, who took human form. When she licked him, however, she left a patch of fur. Oisín became one of the heroes of Fianna.

Blathnat: Irish goddess and daughter of the Irish faery king Midir. Sometimes she's also mentioned as the daughter of the mortal king Concobar Mac Nessa. She has magical cattle and a magic cauldron. Her name means "little flower," and many believe that she is linked to the Welsh Blodeuwedd.

Blondine: The only surviving folktale of Blondine comes from Brittany—a story that is full of clues suggesting she is a faery queen or a goddess who was diminished. It features a well that is said to be mirror-bright, as well as magical rings, magical crows, spells of forgetfulness, and finally reunited love. Sometimes she is called Velandinenn or Princess Velandinnen.

Bó Dhu: Black cow goddess who arose with her sisters from the sea. She traveled south to populate Ireland with cows.

Bó Find: Irish goddess who is said to have risen from the sea in the west and, along with her sisters, populated Ireland with cows. She may be the same figure as Bóand, as she sometimes appears as a white cow.

Bó Ruadh: Red cow goddess who arose from the sea with her sister. She traveled north and helped to populate Ireland with cows.

Bóand/Boann: Irish goddess whose name means "white cow," "shining cow," or "woman of the white cow." Although no cows appear in any of the surviving stories or legends, some scholars believe that she may be the same as Bó Find. The River Boyne is named after her and she is associated with a forbidden well. Sometimes she is called Eithne.

Bochtóg: Irish faery woman who saved people from drowning when they fell asleep during a rising tide. She is described as beautiful, with long blond hair.

Branwen: Welsh goddess whose story is recorded in *The Mabinogi.* Her name means "white raven." She is the daughter of Llyr, sister to Brân the Blessed, and half sister to Efnisien. She was married to the Irish king Matholwch, which angered Efnisien, so he slaughtered the king's horses, forcing Branwen into humiliating servitude. She befriended a starling who carried a letter home to Wales on its leg, prompting Brân to attempt to free her. But he was killed and Branwen died of a broken heart.

Bréifine: Obscure Irish goddess whose name is sometimes spelled Breffni. She is connected with sovereignty, warrior women, and defending the land.

Brenhines-y-Nef: Obscure ancient Welsh goddess considered to be the ancestral mother with strong maternal powers. She may be a sky goddess.

Bricta/Brixia: Consort of Luxovius associated with the sacred spring at Luxeuli in Haute-Saône in France. She may be linked to Brighid and has associations with healing.

Brigindo: Goddess from Gaul who may be connected with Brighid or Brigantia.

Britannia: British goddess who is believed to be the personification of Britain. She represents the sovereignty of the British landscape.

Bronach: The name of a 6th-century Irish holy woman and mystic.

Bronwen: Obscure Welsh goddess that many people believe is the original goddess in Welsh stories of Branwen. However, others strongly disagree and believe that they are completely separate beings. Her name, which means "white-bosomed," is also the name of a mountain in the north of Wales named White Breast. She is associated with the faery folk, the color white, the Cauldron of Regeneration, and becoming the bridge.

Brunissen: Obscure Celtic goddess who is preserved in French fairy tales. She is connected with the Brocéliande Forest, which has a long history of magical stories. Her name means "Brown Queen."

Buanann: Obscure Irish goddess who is briefly mentioned as the mother of heroes and may have a connection to abundance.

Caer Ibormeith: Daughter of the Irish mythological Prince Ethal Anbuail and the beloved of Aonhus óg. She had the ability to shapeshift and turned into a human for a day every alternate Samhain at sunset. Then she reverted back to her original form as a swan.

Caíntigern: Obscure Irish goddess who is the daughter of Manannán Mac Lir and mother of King Mongán.

Cairenn: Irish heroine who is possibly a goddess who was the protector of children.

Cally Berry: Irish weather spirit portrayed as a malignant supernatural hag. She is similar to the Cailleach Bhéara (Irish).

Cana Cludhmor/Canola: Irish goddess of music said to have invented the harp from a whale bone.

Caolainn: Obscure Irish goddess associated with the healing well in County Roscommon. She clawed her own eyes out and then crawled to the healing well, where she healed herself and her eyes grew back.

Carlin: Scottish goddess associated with The Cailleach.

Carman: Irish goddess who ruled Ireland. Her three sons were Dub, which means darkness, Dian, which means violence, and Dothur, which means wickedness. They ruined Ireland's crops until Danu and the Tuatha Dé Danann stopped them.

Cathleen ni Houlihan: Irish sovereignty goddess with associations similar to The Cailleach.

Cathubodua: Gaelic warrior goddess. Only a single Gallo-Roman inscription of her survives, found in Savoy. Her name means "battle raven" and she may be connected to Badb. She is associated with fighting, violence, fury, and rage.

Ceibhfhionn/Cabfin: Irish goddess associated with wisdom and inspiration who was said to stand near the Well of Wisdom with a sacred vessel.

Cethlion: Irish goddess associated with prophecy and foresight who was said to have buckteeth

Cigfa: Welsh goddess who married Rhiannon's son, Pryderi.

Clíodhna: Irish goddess of the Otherworld and queen of the banshees who is sometimes seen as a goddess of love and beauty. She had magical birds that were said to eat the apples of the Otherworld and could sing the sick to sleep so they could be healed. She is also associated with the ninth wave, the ninth and largest wave in a series being called "Clídna's wave." She was also associated with the faery hill Carrig Cliodna in Cork and was originally believed to be a goddess of the land. She is sometime seen as a sea faery. She turned Aeval into a white cat.

Clota: Scottish goddess associated with the River Clyde, said to be associated with fertility.

Conaran: Obscure Irish goddess who was the mother of three magical daughters.

Corra: Irish goddess who is sometimes seen as a mother goddess. In other cases, she is called a serpent goddess and is linked with the mythology of Saint Patrick.

Creiddylad: Welsh goddess who is the daughter of Lludd. She is associated with Beltane. Later, Shakespeare transforms her into Cordelia, the daughter of Lear.

Creirwy: Cerridwen's daughter and a Breton saint from 16th-century Wales.

Crobh Dearg: Irish goddess associated with Munster and with Saint Gobnat. She may be the same goddess as Badb and has associations with the holy well near the Paps of Danu. Her name means "red claw."

Cuda: Obscure British goddess associated with Cirencester. Her sacred association is an egg.

Cymidei Cymeinfoll: Giantess who emerged from a lake every six weeks to birth a fully grown and armed warrior. She is a goddess of regeneration and war, and her name means "bloated with war."

Dames Vertes: French elemental spirits who have clear ties to faery women and may be diminished goddesses. They were said to lurk in forests and lure and torture travelers in nearby water-

falls. In Britain, they are called the Green Ladies and have been compared to mermaids.

Damona: Goddess found in continental Europe whose name means "divine cow." She shares similarities with Bóand. Alternatively, she is sometimes seen as a goddess of sheep. Dedications have been found to her near sacred wells in Alesia. Her sacred associations are corn and snakes, which indicates that she is a fertility or prosperity goddess.

Dea Nutrix: Nursing goddess or goddesses associated with Celtic mother goddesses like Matrona or the Matres. They are linked to fertility and have sacred associations with eggs, children, fruit, and grains.

Dee: British goddess associated with the River Dee. Her name means "the goddess."

Delbáeth: Obscure Irish goddess mentioned in the Irish *Book of Invasions*. Her name means either "fire-shaped" or "enchanted fire."

Dér Gréine: Goddess associated with both Scotland and Ireland whose name means "tears of the sun."

Devona: Continental Celtic goddess associated with springs and rivers. Her name means "stream goddess."

Digne: Irish ancestral goddess of Munster who is connected to The Cailleach.

Donand: Obscure Irish goddess who is mentioned in the Irish *Book of Invasions*. She shares many attributes with Danu and is often conflated with her, alhough it is argued that they are distinctive figures.

Dubinn: Obscure Irish goddess.

Eblinne: Irish mountain goddess.

Echtach: Irish goddess who takes the form of an owl and haunts County Clare. She is sister to Echthge.

Echthge: Irish goddess who is the daughter of Nuada. She was said to have eaten her children, earning her the reputation of a cannibal goddess. Her name means "terrible goddess," "the awful one," or "awful daughter."

Erce: Obscure British or Germanic goddess who is considered a Mother Earth goddess. Her name means "exalted one."

Eriu: Personification of Ireland and mother goddess.

Ernmas: Obscure Irish goddess who is the mother of Fódla, Eiru, and Banba. She is also sometimes mentioned as the mother of the three goddesses who make up the triune goddess The Morrigan. Her name translates as either "death by weapons" or "iron."

Etáin: Irish warrior queen who is sometimes also identified as a sun goddess and whose name means "swift one." There are many Irish figures who have names similar to hers or bear her name, which can cause much confusion. She is sometimes conflated with Epona.

Etan: Irish goddess of crafts.

Fand: Also Fann. Faery queen married to Manannán Mac Lir. Her name means "tear."

Féthnat: Obscure Irish goddess and one of the Tuathe Dé Danann.

Fial: Irish goddess associated with the River Feale. She is believed to be a goddess of fertility and abundance.

Finnen: Faery queen and Irish goddess. Her name means "brilliant" or "white." She is possibly the twin sun goddess to Áine.

Flidais: Irish goddess whose name means "doe." She is associated with deer and supernatural herds, drove a chariot pulled by deer, and had a magical cow.

Fodla: One of the three goddess of Ireland, along with Banbha and Eriu.

Gillagréine: Obscure Irish goddess whose mother was a sunbeam.

Glastig: Scottish and Welsh faery woman who may be a diminished goddess. Sometimes associated with The Cailleach, her name means "water hag." She has the upper body of a woman and lower body of a goat. She is said to haunt forgotten lakes and pools, and is sometimes described as beautiful and sometimes as haggard. She is associated with the Cailleach Bheurra.

Gobnat: Irish goddess linked to Sheela Na Gig. She is associated with Saint Gobnait, who was the patroness of bees.

Gráinne: Irish goddess and daughter of Cormac. Her story is found in the Book of Leinster.

Grian: Irish sun goddess associated with the winter sun.

Guinevere: Arthurian figure and wife of King Arthur who is sometimes venerated by her devotees as a goddess. There is evidence that King Arthur married three different Guineveres, which strengthens her role as a goddess and possibly even as a triple or triune goddess. Some versions of her story parallel Gráinne's story, as well as that of Iseult.

Gwyar: Welsh goddess who is known as the wife of the God of Heaven. She is sometimes said to be the sister to King Arthur.

Habetrot: British spinner goddess who has been diminished to a faery queen, faery woman, or folkloric figure. She had the power to weave fabric that, when turned into clothing, protected against illness. She is thus considered a healing goddess.

Habondia: Celtic or Germanic abundance and fertility goddess who was worshiped in the Roman era. In the 13th-century Roman de la Rose, she is known as Habonde. Later, Pierre de Lancre demotes her to a queen of fae, a nymph, or a sybil. She is goddess of the River Liffey and the plains around it.

Henwen: In Welsh legend, a sow who gave birth to Cath Palug, a monstrous cat depicted as combatting either Sir Kay or King Arthur in Arthurian tales. Her name means "old white." Her sacred associations are wheat, barley, bees, wolf cub, kitten, and eagle. If you have seen the animated film *The Black Cauldron*, you may already be familiar with Henwen.

Ianuaria: Obscure goddess from Burgundy who was worshiped at the Roman-Celtic healing spring at Beire-le-Châtel.

Icauna: Continental Celtic goddess who presided over the land and rivers. She is the tutelary goddess of the River Yonne in France.

Icovellauna: Obscure goddess who was worshiped in Gaul. Inscriptions to her are found in Trier, Germany, and she is believed to be connected to water. An octagonal shrine to her was found at the Sablon Spring.

Igraine: Arthurian heroine who is said to be the mother of King Arthur and Morgan le Fae.

Ile: Scottish goddess for whom the Isle of Islay in the Hebrides is named.

Inghean Bhuidhe: Irish goddess known as the yellow-haired one who is possibly a fire goddess like her sister, Latiaran. She was later turned into a Christian saint and honored on May 6 at a holy well.

Ioua: Scottish goddess thought to be connected to the moon for whom the Isle of Iona is named.

Januaria: Continental Celtic goddess found at a single healing shrine in Burgundy. She is associated with music and healing.

Jenny Greenteeth: Water spirit who is most likely a diminished water goddess or faery woman. She is associated with streams in Lancashire and is now known worldwide. She is often associated with swamps.

Lair Derg: Irish goddess whose name means "red mare," which may connect her with Áine.

Lasair: Obscure Irish goddess associated with holy wells. Her festival is April 18.

Latiaran: Irish goddess who is associated with a heart-shaped standing stone found in the small town of Cullen in County Cork. She is also associated with holy wells.

Lí Ban: Irish mermaid goddess whose name means "beauty of womanhood."

Litavis: Obscure continental goddess associated with the earth.

Mal: Irish hag goddess.

Medb: Irish goddess who is most commonly known as Queen Medb, but is sometimes called Maeve. She is sometimes linked with Badb or The Morrigan. Her name is linked with mead and means "intoxication." She was later diminished into a Welsh faery queen and appears in Shakespeare's *Romeo and Juliet* as Queen Mab.

Milucra: Irish goddess who is sister to Áine.

Mór: Irish goddess whose name translates as "large" or "great." She is a land goddess who was later diminished into a folkloric figure.

Morgause: Arthurian figure usually portrayed as the daughter of Igraine and sister to Morgan. She is also the mother of Mordred and lived in Orkney.

Nás: Obscure Irish goddess and wife of Ludd.

Natosuelta: Continental Celtic goddess associated with water. Her name means "winding brook," or "meandering river." She is a river goddess whose sacred associations are a bowl or pot and a raven. Some suggest that she is a goddess of the hearth.

Nehalennia: Continental Celtic goddess who may be associated with Elen of the Ways.

Nemain: Irish goddess who is one of the three figures who make up The Morrigan. Her name means "battle panic."

Nemausicae: Set of fertility and healing goddesses found in France who are connected to the Matres. Sometimes called Matres Nemausicae.

Nerthus: Germanic goddess who may have Celtic roots or associations.

Nessa: Irish goddess and mother of King Concobar Mac Nessa. Assa means "gentle one" and through her story it transforms to "Nessa the ungentle."

Niamh: Irish faery queen.

Nimue: Arthurian figure of Otherworldly origin who is sometimes called the Lady of the Lake. She is also known as

the lover of Merlin, and may be conflated with Morgause or Viviane.

Ogniad: Irish goddess or faery queen who is the daughter of Midir and mother of Sigmall. She was known to be lawless and governed by her own will.

Olwen: Daughter of a giantess whose name means "white footprint." Her colors are red, yellow, and white. She is associated with white clover, white flowers, and the trefoil knot known as the triquetra. She may be a diminished sun goddess.

Peg Powler: A diminished form of a river goddess associated with the River Tees near Yorkshire.

Penarddun: Welsh figure and daughter of Dôn and Beli.

Ragnell: Arthurian figure who may be a diminished goddess. She is the wife of Fwain and has the ability to shapeshift. She is known as the Loathly Lady who can transform into a hag or a beautiful woman. As such, she is sometimes conflated with The Cailleach.

Ratis: Continental Celtic goddess and protector of forts.

Rigani: Continental Celtic goddess whose name translates as "Great Queen." There is some evidence that she is connected to Rosmerta.

Ritona: Obscure goddess from Gaul who is associated with fords and rivers.

Ruad: Irish goddess who is associated with waterfalls.

Sabrina/Hafren: British goddess, nymph, and historical figure. She is goddess of the River Severn, which is the largest river in the United Kingdom. Some believe that she is both a nymph and a goddess, but the *Historia Regum Britanniae* describes her as a

Cornish princess whose parents were drowned in the Severn and this may be where her identity as a nymph originated.

Saitada: An obscure goddess that is associated with suffering and grief. Her worship was in the Tyne Valley near Hadrian's Wall.

Senach: Obscure Irish goddess who has magical power over time.

Sequana: Goddess of the River Seine, particularly the springs that are its source, which are located in Burgundy. A healing shrine dating back to the 1st or 2nd century BCE was established here that was later taken over by the Romans. Wooden and stone images of limbs, internal organs, heads, and even complete bodies were offered to her here in the hope of a cure, as well as coins and items of jewelry.

Sheela na Gig: A figure who represents the Divine Feminine. She is often portrayed with her legs splayed and is sometimes seen as an aspect or representation of the hag goddesses.

Sinann: Irish goddess and granddaughter of Lir.

Sirona: Celtic healing goddess worshiped predominantly in east-central Gaul and along the Danube. She was associated with healing springs.

Souconna: Obscure continental Celtic goddess associated with the River Saône in France.

Suleviae: Triune mother goddess associated with sun worship and healing. May be connected to Sulis, but others argue they are completely separate.

Tailtiu: Irish goddess and foster mother of Lugh.

Tamara: Diminished goddess from Cornwall and Britain who is now s een as a nymph of the River Tamar, which flows between Cornwall and Devon.

Telo: Continental Celtic goddess who is associated with a healing spring in Toulon, France.

Triduana: Scottish goddess or saint associated with the number three who may be similar to Saint Brigit.

Verbia: British river goddess associated with the River Warfe whose name translates as "she of the cattle." She is said to apprear on May 1 in the form of a white horse or cow.

Visucia: Obscure continental Celtic goddess to whom several inscriptions have been found in France.

Vivian: Arthurian figure and possibly a diminished goddess who is sometimes conflated with Nimue and is known to be the lover of Merlin. She is most often thought of as a faery woman.

Warna: Obscure Cornish goddess worshiped by mariners. She was honored on the Isle of Scilly near Cornwall and is also connected to a sacred well there.

Washer at the Ford: Faery woman connected with several goddesses, including Nicnevin, Black Anis, and The Morrigan. She is often seen washing the clothes of those who are about to die in battle.

White Ladies: Faery women said to be connected to sacred wells and other bodies of water. Sightings of these white ladies abound. They could be water nymphs, spirits of rivers and wells, or diminished water goddesses.

APPENDIX B

Index of Exercises and Rituals

Chapter 4: Celtic Rituals and Devotional Practices
Seeking Wisdom in the Standing Stones
Building an Altar or Sacred Space
Consecrating, Dedicating, and Anointing a Sacred Image
Anointing, Dressing, and Blessing Sacred Candles
Finding and Consecrating a Sacred Vessel
Celtic Goddess Simmer Pot
Celtic Goddess Incense
Celtic Goddess Bath Soak

Chapter 5: Sulis—Goddess of the Gap
Honoring Sulis
Sulis Spell Bottle
Sunrise with Sulis
Spell to Seek Sulis's Blessing
Solar Tea Ritual
Sulis Ritual Bath
Quick Healing Ritual

Chapter 6: Brighid—Goddess of the Sacred Well
Invocation to Brighid
Clootie Ritual for Healing
Saining in Brighid's Name
Bridie's Bed
Creating a Brighid's Cross
Brighid's Mantle

Chapter 7: Arnemetia and Nemetona—Goddesses of the Sacred Grove
Forest Ritual to Honor Arnemetia
Making a Wild Necklace to Honor Nemetona
Journey to Nemetona's Sacred Grove

Chapter 8: Coventina—Goddess of the Sacred Spring
Petition for Healing
Petition to Protect the Spirits of the Dead
Creating an Ancestor Altar

Chapter 9: Elen of the Ways—The Antlered Goddess
Invocation to Elen
Road-Building Meditation

Chapter 10: Melusine—Mermaid Goddess of the Fount
Sacred Bath to Seek Melusine's Blessing
Beauty Bath
Charm Rings

Chapter 11: The Cailleach—Giantess
Using Storm Water for Protection
Harvest Spirit Doll

Chapter 12: The Matres
Healing the Mother Wound
Charm Bag for Fertility

BIBLIOGRAPHY

Allason-Jones, Lindsay and Bruce McKay. *Coventina's Well*. Oxford, England: Trustees of the Clayton Collection, 1985.

Arras, Jean d'. *Melusine or the Noble History of Lusignan*. Trans., Donald Maddox and Sara Sturm-Maddox. University Park, PA: Pennsylvania State University Press, 2012.

Campbells, John Gregorson. *The Gaelic Otherworld: John Gregorson Campbell's Superstitions of the Highlands and the Islands of Scotland and Witchcraft and Second Sight in the Highlands and the Islands*. Edinburgh: Origin, 2008.

Davies, Sioned. *Mabinogi*. New York: Oxford University Press, 2007.

Dexter, Miriam Robbins. "Reflections on the Goddess Danu." *Mankind Quarterly*, vol. XXXI, nos. 1 & 2, Fall/Winter 1990.

Fear, A. T. "Bladud: The Flying King of Bath." *Folklore*, vol. 103, no. 2, 1992, pp. 222–24.

Gose, Erich. *Der Tempelbezirk des Lenus Mars in Trier*. Berlin: Gebr. Mann, 1955.

Green, Miranda J. *Dictionary of Celtic Myth and Legend*. New York: Thames amd Hudson, 1992.

Heurgon, Jacques. Review of Erich Gose's *Der Tempelbezirk des Lenus Mars in Trier. The Journal of Roman Studies*, vol. 47, no. 1/2, 1957, pp. 281–82.

King, Melanie. *The Secret History of English Spas*. Oxford, UK: Bodleian Library, 2021.

McHardy, Stuart. *Quest for the Nine Maidens*. Trowbridge: Cromwell Press, 2003.

McNeill, F. Marian. *The Silver Bough*. Edinburgh, Scotland: Conongate Classic, 1956.

Monaghan, Patrica. *Encyclopedia of Celtic Mythology and Folklore*. New York: Facts on File Inc., 2004.

Rankine, David and Sorita d'Este. *Visions of the Cailleach: Exploring the Myths, Folklore and Legends of the Pre-eminent Celtic Hag Goddess*. London: Avalonia, 2009.

Ray, Rebecca Celeste. *Sacred Waters: A Cross-Cultural Compendium of Hallowed Springs and Holy Wells*. London: Routledge, 2020.

Revell, Louise. "Religion and Ritual in the Western Provinces." *Greece & Rome*, vol. 54, no. 2, 2007, pp. 210–28.

Robbins, Miriam. "Reflections on the Goddess Donu." *The Mankind Quarterly*, vol. XXXI, nos. 1 & 2, Fall/Winter 1990.

Sigel, Carlie. "Exhibition Paper for the Genius Cucullatus." Archived August 4, 2007, *The Wayback Machine*.

Wightman, Edith Mary. *Roman Trier and the Treveri*. London: Rupert Hart-Davis, 1970.

Wise, Caroline. *Finding Elen—The Quest for Elen of the Ways*. London: Eala Press, 2015.

INDEX